PS Advisory Bc Member's Note

MW00658064

MARK CLIFFE
Chief Economist of the ING Group

"(De)Reconstruction," the theme of this special year-end magazine issue, captures the current global turmoil as we enter a new decade. While longstanding geopolitical arrangements, political norms, business models, and even mainstream economic theories are under strain or unraveling, efforts are already underway to create a new foundation for global peace and prosperity.

AS I POINTED OUT IN 2018, economists who continue to ignore the far-reaching disruptions that are underway do so at their peril. The years since the global financial crisis have exposed fundamental flaws in mainstream macroeconomic thinking. We are living in a world of deep structural instability and uncertainty, in which policymakers have had no choice but to look for new policy tools.

As in previous years, the major central banks struggled to hit their inflation targets in 2019, even amid low or declining unemployment. After moving toward monetary-policy normalization, the US Federal Reserve has since switched gears, cutting its policy rate. Meanwhile, the European Central Bank has launched another round of asset purchases to accompany interest-rate cuts. And yet, the long-term effects – politically, economically, or otherwise – of a decade of unconventional monetary policies have yet to reveal themselves fully.

More broadly, social and political upheavals, technological change, rising inequality within countries, and an impending climate crisis all demand that economists challenge their own assumptions, and that businesses rethink how they operate. For its part, the Business Roundtable, an organization of CEOs of leading American corporations, announced in August that its members now favor abandoning shareholder primacy and shifting to a multi-stakeholder model of corporate governance. And a growing number of companies are making commitments to reduce their carbon footprints, with many coalescing around the target of net-zero carbon emissions by 2050. But it remains to be seen if they can translate ambitious words into effective action.

Much will depend on the broader policy context, and whether global-governance institutions can reclaim the mantle of effective multilateralism. While populist governments around the world have continued to run up public debts to pay for handouts to their supporters, traditional liberals, Greens, and others arc pushing back. How these political contests play out will depend both on the economy and on debates over identity; how our long-term economic prospects fare will depend on our politics. With the Trump presidency, Brexit, the Sino-American battle for tech supremacy, and other global frictions we have left one world behind. But we do not yet know what will come next. This will become clearer in 2020. PS

Mark Cliffe is Chief Economist of the ING Group.

PS.(De)Reconstruction

Project Syndicate

Editors' Introduction

Populist and nationalist disruptions continued apace in 2019. Even with a "deal," US President Donald Trump's trade war with China has rattled businesses around the world, and seems to be inciting a highly disruptive process of deglobalization as escalating protectionism impels companies to seek to reshore production and keep supply chains closer to home. This danger coincides with already-fragile global economic growth. Europe and many other regions are nearing recession, and a downturn in the United States is widely expected. And when the next recession does arrive, economic policymakers will have few tools to counter it. The major central banks are largely powerless to stimulate the economy, and government debt worldwide is at a record high.

US PRESIDENT DONALD TRUMP AND INDIAN PRIME MINISTER NARENDRA MODI AT THE WHITE HOUSE.

As policymakers from Washington, DC, to Beijing well know, the future is now up for grabs."

AS IN THE DECADE FOLLOWING THE 2008 financial crisis, another economic crash could have far-reaching political consequences. The future of liberal democracy already appears at risk. In the US, the report by Special Counsel Robert Mueller, which revealed ample evidence of Trump's attempts to obstruct justice, and of his presidential campaign's delight at the help it received from a hostile foreign power, was duly forgotten within weeks. Yet in the ensuing months, new evidence of Trump's abuses of power continued

to pile up. With Democrats in the House of Representatives having now launched a formal impeachment inquiry, continued partisan gridlock in Washington, DC – potentially leading to yet another government shutdown – seems all but assured.

In the United Kingdom, Boris Johnson's arrival in 10 Downing Street soon put a deeply polarized country on the verge of a constitutional crisis. Even if the UK government, more than three years after the Brexit referendum, can secure an agreement to withdraw from the European Union, the more difficult work of negotiating a new relationship with Europe and the rest of the world will have only just begun.

▲ SPEAKER OF THE US HOUSE OF REPRESENTATIVES NANCY PELOSI.

▶ BRITISH PRIME MINISTER BORIS JOHNSON.

The rise of populists like Trump and Johnson was fueled in part by the growing – and still largely unchecked – power of social media and its weaponization by political candidates and campaigns. More broadly, the role of digital platforms in the political economy of all countries continued to raise concerns in 2019. In addition to announcing plans to launch its own private currency, Facebook also signaled that it would continue to allow disinformation – including political ads based on lies – to flow freely on its network. And while a number of US tech IPOs this year undershot expectations – or, in the case of WeWork, went up in flames – the dominant players in Silicon Valley and Shenzhen continued to lock down their near-monopoly positions in cloud computing, artificial intelligence, and other key sectors of the twenty-first-century economy.

But while the post-war international order has been irreparably damaged in recent years, it remains to be seen what will come next. Populist excesses have triggered a growing counter-movement. The EU, at least, is stepping up to rein in the power of Big Tech, salvage nuclear diplomacy in the Middle East, and maintain the consensus on addressing climate change. In Asia, Japanese Prime Minister Shinzo Abe has revived the Trans-Pacific Partnership, after Trump's withdrawal of the US left the mega-regional trade deal all but dead, and is working on forging new regional security and trade arrangements capable of counterbalancing China in the absence of American leadership. And young people around the world have joined movements demanding climate action and democratic governance.

As policymakers from Washington, DC, to Beijing well know, the future is now up for grabs. With populists having suffered setbacks in 2019 in Hungary, Israel, Romania, Slovakia, Turkey, and in the European Parliament elections, there is hope yet that a democratic wave will roll back the authoritarian tide in 2020. The outcome of the US presidential election in November 2020 will no doubt be a bellwether: Trump's re-election would embolden strongmen worldwide, while leaving in ruins whatever multilateral mechanisms could rein them in. But, as the contributions to *The Year Ahead 2020* make clear, even if democratic forces win out, the hard work of building a sustainable, inclusive, and prosperous global order will still lie ahead. **PS**

Richard Eames
Roman Frydman
Kenneth Murphy
Jonathan Stein
Stuart Whatley

Can a Political-Economy Vicious Circle Be Avoided?

LAWRENCE H. SUMMERS
University Professor at Harvard University

(De)Reconstruction

Domestic politics, geopolitics, and economics will be intertwined in 2020 to an extent unmatched in decades. Weak economic performance and problematic governance in much of the world risks setting in motion a vicious circle: adverse economic outcomes lead to populism at home and truculent nationalism abroad, which in turn exacerbate economic problems as protectionism increases, investment declines, and consumer confidence falls off. Bad economics drives bad politics, leading to worse economics and worse politics.

BOTH THE BAD NEWS AND THE GOOD news is that economics and politics will start 2020 in a parlous state. The global economy could fall into recession, and the risk of major political or even military confrontation is higher than it has been since the end of the Cold War. From a more optimistic perspective, with expectations very low, it will not take much to generate positive surprises that could lead to a virtuous circle of economic improvement and less toxic politics.

Start with the economics. The International Monetary Fund has coined the term "synchronized slowdown" to refer to our current predicament: growth is decelerating in 90% of the world economy and is expected to be slower overall than at any time since the financial crisis. It is a euphemism for the secular stagnation that increasingly characterizes the global economy. In the current climate of slow population growth, rising inequality and high uncertainty about the absorption of saving is a defining problem.

Just as in the 1930s, the advanced economies are incapable of sustained growth at healthy rates with a sound financial and policy foundation. Markets expect that central banks will fail to achieve their 2% inflation targets over the next decade. Even to achieve what electorates see as inadequate growth in middle-class standards of living, the world has had to issue $15 trillion in negative interest-rate debt, run unprecedentedly large peacetime budget deficits, and allow various financial excesses to go unchecked.

While emerging markets represent a far larger share of the global economy than they have historically done, and came through the financial crisis with more resilience than most would have expected, their success remains dependent on the developed countries. The most successful emerging-market growth trajectories have been based on exports of manufactured goods to growing developed economies. A combination of slowing growth, reshoring of manufacturing, and rising protectionism means that this route to growth will be increasingly difficult in the years ahead. Forecasts of emerging-market growth have been consistently too optimistic ▶

▶ DONALD TRUMP ADDRESSES THE INTERNATIONAL ASSOCIATION OF CHIEFS OF POLICE.

in recent years, and I fear this will continue. China, in particular, faces profound structural challenges in the years ahead.

Judged purely on their own terms, these economic challenges would be considered serious, though perhaps not more so than the oil shocks or great inflation or financial crises of the past. What makes the current challenges worse is the deterioration almost everywhere in the capacity for a reasoned response. Under President Donald Trump, the United States, which underwrote the international system that won the Cold War and allowed emerging markets to converge toward developed-country living standards, has embraced an atavistic notion of perpetual struggle between nation-states and is leading a worldwide retreat from global integration. Whether the issue is trade agreements, cooperation on issues like climate change, or support for human rights, the US is reliably absent.

It is tempting to blame Trump, and he has rarely if ever missed a chance to blunder. But it should be remembered that until Trump withdrew the US from the Trans-Pacific Partnership trade deal, more Democrats than Republicans opposed the TPP, and that the Democrats' presidential candidate in the 2020 election is likely to attack Trump's policies toward China as overly conciliatory. In a sense, the post-World War II consensus on American leadership ended with President Barack Obama's observation that his grand strategy could be boiled down to "Don't do stupid shit."

More fundamentally, the nationalist turn we have seen in the US is just one manifestation of a global trend that encompasses Brexit; populist governments in Italy, Hungary, Poland, Mexico, Brazil, and the Philippines; and rising ethnic nationalism in Turkey, India, and China, not to mention Russia after 20 years of Vladimir Putin's rule. Decision-making based on reason, sound economics, and international cooperation is being overwhelmed by a wave of popular anger and nationalist fantasy.

More resistance to globally integrated markets, reduced foreign investment, and less international cooperation can only mean slower economic growth and more insecurity and

"Worldwide, the single most important choice made in 2020 will be that of US voters in the presidential election."

► SUPPORTERS OF MEXICO'S NEW PRESIDENT, ANDRÉS MANUEL LÓPEZ OBRADOR.

(De)Reconstruction

frustration for working people. They will then be much more likely to rally behind those with the simplest stories and the most expansive promises than to support a return to centrist cooperative policies. This will only deepen the economic malaise.

These dynamics are not confined to democracies. If Russia's economy were delivering for Russians, there would be much less need for Putin's increasing concentration of power. It is no accident that decelerating growth and rising risks to financial instability in China have coincided with greater repression of dissent, crackdowns on minorities, and appeals to nationalism. Perhaps the massive military display that accompanied the celebrations marking the 70th anniversary of the People's Republic – a spectacle that dwarfed the commemoration of previous anniversaries – was as much a reflection of insecurity as of confidence.

Worldwide, the single most important choice made in 2020 will be that of US voters in the presidential election. A course correction is more important than at any time in American history. The US and the world need a new

▲ DEMOCRATIC PRESIDENTIAL CANDIDATES DEBATE IN WESTERVILLE, OHIO.

president who prizes community over confrontation in pursuit of inclusive prosperity at home and abroad. This means focusing on necessary public investments in infrastructure, education, and innovation; making the tax code more efficient and progressive; and focusing businesses on meeting society's needs rather than fomenting a war between labor and business or the middle class and the rich.

It also means ending the current US trade war against most of the world, ceasing the use of capriciousness to generate leverage, and dropping the use of diplomacy to pursue domestic political aims. The right focus is to restore US alliances, resist protectionism, and join with other countries to address global challenges such as climate change, tax evasion, and the regulation of new technologies.

A change in what America exemplifies, the policies it pursues, and how it influences the rest of the world is probably necessary to avoid a vicious political/economic circle. The degree of change in the global environment after Franklin D. Roosevelt's election during the Great

Depression, Ronald Reagan's election during a period of self-doubt in the West, and Obama's election after the Iraq War and in the midst of a financial crisis suggests that US elections have profound consequences for the global system. People watch and emulate the city on a hill. For better or worse, that will be true in 2020 as well. ▨

Lawrence H. Summers was US Secretary of the Treasury (1999–2001), Director of the US National Economic Council (2009–2010), and President of Harvard University (2001–2006), where he currently is University Professor.

Demagogi

Constitutio

(De)Reconstruction

Stress and

nal Growth

LAURENCE TRIBE
*University Professor at
Harvard Law School*

The United States is living through a remarkably convulsive period in its history. Donald Trump has reshaped the American presidency, and his norm-shattering behavior has tested the US Constitution in profound ways. He has placed stress on points of constitutional vulnerability, particularly when it comes to judicially unenforceable norms of respect for fact-based reality, for orderly decision-making, and for investigatory and prosecutorial independence.

TRUMP'S RISE TO POWER HAS ALSO raised questions about some of the Constitution's most solidly entrenched provisions. His victory in 2016 highlighted the dangers posed by the Electoral College in the face of changing demographic realities, and now his presidency is testing the viability of the impeachment process to cope with a demagogue who has captured the machinery of an entire political party and controls one chamber of Congress.

Some have argued that the Trump presidency represents no more than a mere "blip" in American history. Justice Ruth Bader Ginsburg believes that historians will view our current moment as no more than "an aberration." Others have suggested similar notions, characterizing the question of Trump's long-term impact on American politics and society as up for debate. The arc of history is long, go such arguments, and this presidency will look much smaller in the rear-view mirror than it does today.

I doubt that. In my view, we are living through a transformative moment in American life. Trump has reshaped the contents of American constitutionalism, doubtless in ways he cannot begin to comprehend. Even if the precise nature of that reshaping remains to be determined, the US Constitution will never be the same.

That is not solely a commentary on the harm Trump might do, or the hope he might reveal. Rather, it is a testament to the organic nature of America's founding document and of the institutional matrix that frames it. The Constitution is less a fixed "thing" than a process of creation and re-creation, an intergenerational project of stress and growth. Trump, without remotely appreciating or caring about what he has been doing, has engaged that creative process in transformative ways. And the effects will reverberate through America's legal and social fabric for generations.

An Evolving Framework

Trump's presidency thus reminds us of a fundamental truth about the character of the American constitutional order. Our Constitution has always been an active, participatory enterprise. Only its bare outlines are hard-wired; the rest provides the locus for the spirited, difficult debates that characterize our vibrant republic. This presidency has driven sustained, formative national engagement with those debates. Trump's actions, and the actions taken in response, will in no small part define what the Constitution means for the next generation. This is not just a result of his success in placing judges on the country's federal courts, including the Supreme Court. Trump's constitutional legacy will also reflect his influence on the informal interactions among ordinary citizens and opinion leaders – and of such presuppositions as those undergirding the very idea of the rule of law – that do as much as formal judicial rulings to identify the Constitution's living meaning.

This historical moment has thrust the process of constitutional transformation and innovation to center stage in American political life. Most Americans agree that our national institutions are currently not serving us well. Although there are signs of innovation at the local level, our national legislature is characterized by utter dysfunction. Our federal judiciary is transparently politicized. And this president arrogates to himself ever more power, which he exercises with nearly unchecked abandon. Some even feel increasing skepticism about our Constitution as a whole and wonder if fundamental change is the only answer. In many ways, as Harvard's Danielle Allen has put it, "[w]e are in our Articles of Confederation moment."

As a consequence, constitutional reinterpretation (or amendment) is no longer a quixotic mission on the fringe of our national discourse. Such transformation has become among our public conversation's dominant features. Major political candidates have proposed altering the structure of the Supreme Court. Ranked-choice voting has entered the national discourse. The Overton window for constitutional change has flown wide open.

Perhaps the stress our system is undergoing has helped drive into the mainstream a real hunger to cast off fundamental social and political premises that many find unjust. Or perhaps that hunger was already fighting its way into the mainstream, and this chaotic presidency merely coincides with its ascendancy. In any event, our society seems to be on the precipice of a moment of fundamental social change: a nation on the brink, though of what we do not yet know.

So we live in a moment of intense constitutional pressure. The stakes are almost unimaginably high. And what happens next depends in no small part, but not entirely, on what we fashion for ourselves from this self-inflicted national trauma, an observation that of course requires us to define who "we" are – and whom "we" ought and ought not to become. How the impeachment inquiry currently underway unfolds will no doubt represent a key input into that equation.

The Future Is Unwritten

Just as it seems certain that this presidency will change the course of our nation, it is also uncertain what the result of that change will be. Nor is this the sort of uncertainty that a sufficiently wise scientist could eliminate just by studying enough data and applying suitably sophisticated algorithms. It is not akin to the uncertainty of the next 9.0 earthquake, which might in principle be knowable even if we are unable to do the needed calculations.

This is an uncertainty built into the very idea of free will. The future is ours to fashion, to create.

This moment might inaugurate a return to first principles, a rebirth of the US Constitution's fundamental promises. Perhaps we have an opportunity to rediscover the Constitution's noblest values and extend their promise further than ever before. Or perhaps this moment will have hopelessly undermined our constitutional system, marking the culmination of an age of dysfunction, the inflection point in a national turn toward ruin. Unlike the future that Supreme Court Justice Felix Frankfurter once described as hidden in the womb of time, the future of our constitutional journey is hidden because we have yet to choose it.

Among the things I hope this traumatic national period can achieve is a more honest confrontation with our deeply troubling past, and a fuller acknowledgment that the lessons our Constitution has to teach must be the subject of contestation rather than computation. If that happens, our current brush with tyranny will have strengthened us for our next close encounter with genuine

authoritarianism. And in so doing it will have left us better equipped to weather the storms that will continue to batter our republic.

US Supreme Court Justice Robert Jackson famously described the "fixed star[s] in our constitutional constellation." His metaphor feels singularly suggestive in this time of constitutional change. Stars may be "fixed," but the constellations they form are products of human imagination and ingenuity, not cosmologically determined features of the observable universe. So, too, charting our current waters requires human judgment. The Constitution lights the way, but the task of navigation falls to us. And this benighted president has unwittingly sparked debate over how to navigate the ship – by what stars, to what shore, and on whose say-so. We now must seize this moment to look toward a more inclusive horizon, and together decide which points of light are worth following – and which we should release into the darkened night. **PS**

Laurence Tribe is University Professor and Professor of Constitutional Law at Harvard Law School.

▶ JUSTICE RUTH BADER GINSBURG.

◀ JUSTICE ROBERT JACKSON AT THE NUREMBERG TRIALS.

ABHIJIT BANERJEE
2019 Nobel Laureate in Economics

ESTHER DUFLO
2019 Nobel Laureate in Economics

One of the most worrying news stories of 2019 did not receive the coverage one might expect from media outlets in the United States or Europe. But the economic slowdown in China, and the potentially steep deceleration in growth in India, will most likely receive considerably more attention in 2020. ▶

The Other Side

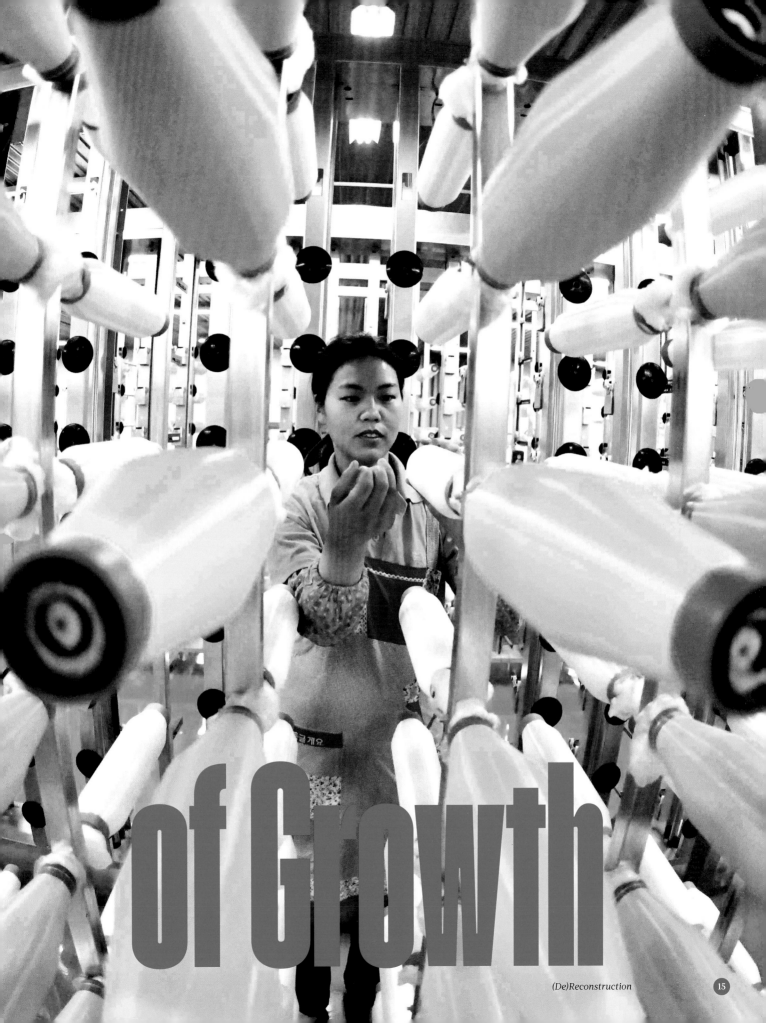

of Growth

THE INTERNATIONAL MONETARY FUND, the Asian Development Bank, and the OECD have downgraded their growth estimates for India in 2019-20 to around 6%, which would be the lowest since the beginning of the decade. Others claim that even this is optimistic and project much more dire narratives. For example, Arvind Subramanian, until recently the Indian government's chief economic adviser, has argued, based on triangulating evidence on various economic indicators, that growth may sink as low as 3.5%.

In China, GDP growth has slowed from 14.2% in 2007 to 6.6% in 2018. The IMF projects that it might fall to 5.5% by 2024. Rapid growth there and in India have lifted millions out of poverty, and the slowdown is likely to impede progress on improving the lives of the poor.

What should China and India do? Or, rather, what should they *not* do? When we were writing our book *Good Economics for Hard Times* in 2018, before the bad news about India starting coming out, we were already concerned about a potential downturn there

(the slowdown in China was already known). Anticipating the fall in growth, we warned that "India should fear complacency."

The point we were making is simple: in countries that start from a situation in which resources are being used badly, as in China under communism or India did in its days of extreme *dirigisme*, the first benefits of reform may come from moving resources to their best uses. In the case of Indian manufacturing firms, for example, there was a sharp acceleration in technological upgrading at the plant level and some reallocation toward the best firms within each industry after 2002. This appears to be unrelated to any changes in economic policy, and has been described as "India's mysterious manufacturing miracle."

But it was no miracle, just a modest improvement from a rather dismal starting point. One can imagine various reasons why it happened. Perhaps it resulted from a generational shift, as control passed from parents to children, often educated abroad, more ambitious, and savvier about technology and world markets. Or maybe the accumulation

The trouble is that countries find it hard to kick the growth habit."

◥ BELT AND ROAD FORUM FOR INTERNATIONAL COOPERATION.

◣ COAL MINES IN INDIA'S EASTERN JHARKAND STATE.

0.5%

JAPAN'S AVERAGE ANNUAL GDP GROWTH RATE BETWEEN 1980–2018.

0.7%

ANNUAL RATE OF DECLINE IN JAPAN'S WORKING-AGE POPULATION SINCE THE LATE 1990S.

of modest profits eventually made it possible to pay for the shift to bigger and better plants. Or maybe both causes – and others – played a role.

More generally, perhaps the reason why some countries, like China, can grow so fast for so long is that they start with a lot of poorly used talent and resources that can be harnessed to more valuable activities. But as the economy sheds its worst plants and firms and solves its most dire misallocation issues, the space for further improvement naturally shrinks. Growth in India, like that in China, had to slow. And there is no guarantee that it will slow only when India has reached the same level of *per capita* income as China. India may be caught in the same "middle-income trap" that ensnared Malaysia, Thailand, Egypt, Mexico, and Peru.

The trouble is that countries find it hard to kick the growth habit. There is a risk that policymakers will flail wildly in their quest to make growth come back. The recent history of Japan should serve as a useful warning.

If Japan's economy had maintained the growth rate that it recorded over the decade 1963–73, it would have

overtaken the US in terms of GDP *per capita* in 1985 and in overall GDP by 1998. What happened instead is enough to make one superstitious: in 1980, the year after Harvard's Ezra Vogel published *Japan as Number One*, the growth rate crashed, and never really recovered. For the entire period 1980–2018, Japan's real GDP grew at an anemic 0.5% average annual rate.

There was a simple problem: low fertility and the near-complete absence of immigration meant Japan was (and is) aging rapidly. The working-age population peaked in the late 1990s, and has been declining at an annual rate of 0.7% ever since (and will continue to decline). Moreover, during the 1950s, 1960s, and 1970s, Japan was catching up after the disaster of the Pacific War, with its well-educated population gradually being deployed to its best possible uses.

By the 1980s, that was over. In the euphoria of the 1970s and 1980s, many people (in Japan and abroad) convinced themselves that Japan would nonetheless sustain rapid growth by inventing new ▶

technologies, which probably explains why the high investment rate (in excess of 30% of GDP) continued through the 1980s. Too much good money chased too few good projects in the so-called bubble economy of the 1980s. As a result, banks ended up with many bad loans, which led to the huge financial crisis of the 1990s. Growth ground to a halt.

At the end of the "lost decade" of the 1990s, Japanese policymakers might have started to realize what was happening and what they had to lose. After all, Japan was already a relatively wealthy economy with much less inequality than most Western economies, a strong education system, and many important problems to address, chief among them how to ensure a decent quality of life for its rapidly aging population. But the authorities appeared unable to adjust: restoring growth was a matter of national pride.

As a result, successive governments vied to devise a series of stimulus packages, spending trillions of dollars mostly on roads, dams, and bridges that served no obvious purpose. Perhaps predictably, the stimulus did nothing to increase economic growth and led to a huge increase in the national debt, to some 230% of GDP in 2016 – by far the highest of the G20 countries and a possible harbinger of a massive debt crisis.

The lesson for policymakers in China and India is clear: they must accept that growth will inevitably slow. China's leaders are aware of it, and have made a conscious effort to manage public expectations accordingly. In 2014, President Xi Jinping talked about a "new normal," of 7% annual growth, rather than 10% or more. But it is not clear that even this projection is realistic, and in the meantime, China is embarking on enormous global construction projects, which doesn't necessarily bode well.

The key, ultimately, is not to lose sight of the fact that GDP is a means and not an end. It is a useful means, no doubt, especially when it creates jobs or raises wages or plumps the government budget so that it can redistribute more. But the ultimate goal remains to raise the average person's – and especially the worst-off person's – quality of life. And quality of life means more than just consumption. Most human beings care about feeling worthy

THE MAIN TERMINAL OF THE NEW BEIJING DAXING INTERNATIONAL AIRPORT.

and respected, and they suffer when they feel that they are failing themselves and their families.

While living better is indeed partly about being able to consume more, even very poor people also care about their parents' health, about their children's education, about having their voices heard, and about being able to pursue their dreams. Higher GDP is only one way to achieve this, and there should be no presumption that it is always the best one.

Many of the important development successes of the last few decades were the direct result of a policy focus on this broader notion of wellbeing, even in some countries that were and have remained very poor. For example, a massive reduction in under-five mortality has occurred even in some very poor countries that were not growing particularly fast, largely thanks to a focus on newborn care, vaccination, and malaria prevention.

This brings us back to the slowdown in India and China. There is a lot that policymakers in both countries can still do to improve the welfare of their citizens and help us cling to some hope about our planet's future. A myopic focus on increasing the rate of GDP growth could squander that chance. PS

Abhijit Banerjee, *Professor of Economics at MIT, is a 2019 Nobel laureate in Economics.*

Esther Duflo, *Professor of Poverty Alleviation and Development Economics at MIT, is a 2019 Nobel laureate in Economics.*

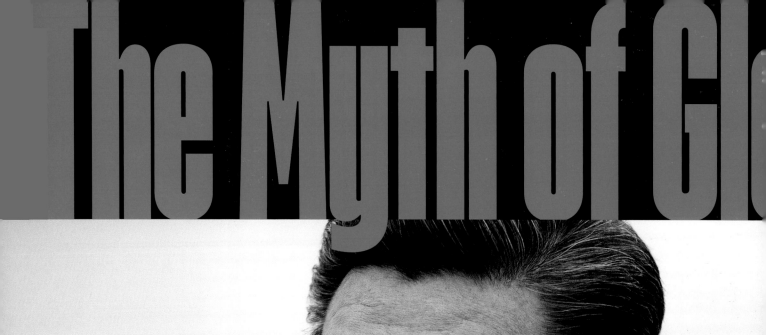

bal Decoupling

Talk of decoupling – a profound and lasting split in the world order – entered public debate in 2019, an alarming manifestation of the mounting conflict between the United States and China. Escalating tit-for-tat tariffs are only the tip of the iceberg. Geostrategic security concerns, early skirmishes in a "tech war," the related fear of two parallel Internets, a nationalistic US president with an overt distaste for "globalism," and a history of military clashes between rising and incumbent powers all raise the specter of a new Iron Curtain reminiscent of the Cold War. ▶

point out that the mounting tensions between the US and China lack the ideological component that many believe was the defining characteristic of the first Cold War. That may be true, but so what? The possibility of a protracted conflict between the world's two largest economies, whatever its cause, should not be taken lightly.

Nevertheless, even if there is a permanent fracture between the US and China, the $87 trillion global economy is unlikely to split into two blocs in 2020 and beyond. The reason is simple: bilateral action cannot divide a tightly linked multilateral trade system.

Today's global economy is far more integrated than ever before. Despite a protracted slowdown of world trade growth in the aftermath of the 2008-09 global financial crisis, trade still stands at around 28% of world GDP. That's essentially double the 13.5% average share in 1947-91, during the Cold War. The tighter that trade is woven into the fabric of global commerce, the tougher it will be to disentangle those linkages – and the lower the odds of a more pervasive and disruptive decoupling.

Moreover, the nature of today's trade linkages makes global decoupling all the more unlikely. Traditional exports and imports of finished goods that were fully produced in individual countries have been increasingly supplanted by fragmented trade in components and parts that are both produced and assembled in a vast network of multi-country global value chains (GVCs). According to a recent study by the International Monetary Fund, the expansion of GVCs accounted for fully 73% of the explosive fivefold growth in global trade between 1993 and 2013. This diffusion of bilateral trade through multi-country supply chains would dampen the effects of a bilateral decoupling of any two economies, no matter how large.

These considerations bear critically on the potential impact of a US-China trade conflict. US politicians like to argue that America's trade problem is a China problem. After all, they say, over the past six years (2013-18), China accounted for 47% of a gaping US merchandise trade deficit. What US politicians don't admit (or understand) is that the

28%

TRADE'S SHARE OF WORLD GDP.

13.5%

TRADE'S AVERAGE SHARE OF WORLD GDP 1947–1991.

overall trade deficit is an outgrowth of America's chronically low net domestic saving rate of just 2.4% of GDP in 2018 – well below the 6.3% average in the final three decades of the twentieth century.

Lacking in saving and wanting to invest and grow, the US must import surplus saving from abroad, running a chronic current-account deficit to attract foreign capital. This macroeconomic imbalance puts China in good company as just one component – albeit a very large one – of America's multilateral deficit in merchandise trade with 102 countries (as of 2018).

Politicians, of course, would be the last to admit that they are the root of the problem, responsible as they are for the chronically large budget deficits that account for the bulk of America's protracted shortfall of domestic saving. Unfortunately, that key feature of America's trade position is likely to be further compounded by the US federal budget outlook, which is going from bad to worse.

The saving shortfall underpinning America's persistent macro imbalances implies that a trade war with China needs to be seen in a different light, and that the decoupling debate should be reframed accordingly. Without addressing the US saving shortfall, raising tariffs and other barriers on China will simply divert trade away from Chinese sourcing toward America's other trading partners. Bilateral decoupling does not mean global decoupling; it means trade diversion.

That diversion will be compounded by global value chains. Based on trade-in-value-added data from the OECD and the World Trade Organization, it turns out that around 20% of the outsize US-China merchandise trade deficit is not made in China; instead, it reflects components, parts, and other inputs from other countries that participate in China-centric supply chains. This suggests that official measures of the US-China bilateral trade deficit are exaggerated, further compromising the rationale for a Chinese solution to America's multilateral trade deficit.

The shift in the structure of trade, from traditional exchange of finished goods produced in individual countries to GVC-driven trade from multiple production platforms, reflects a fundamental

There is a striking irony to a tariff war being instigated by the US, the world's largest deficit saver."

realignment of an increasingly integrated pan-Asian factory. Research reported in the *2019 Global Value Chain Development Report* found that the massive widening of the US-China merchandise trade deficit since China's accession to the WTO in 2001 stems mainly from offshoring to China by other developed countries (especially Japan and Asia's newly industrialized economies such as South Korea and Taiwan). This is very different from the China blame game of which most US politicians are enamored.

As a result, increased GVC connectivity means that tariffs imposed on shipments of finished goods from China to the US will be felt not only by Chinese exporters, but also by third-party countries that are linked to China-centric supply chains. Little wonder, then, that US tariffs are having a broad-based impact, not just on China, but also on other trade-sensitive economies in East Asia. Supply-chain linkages have spread the so-called China fix throughout the region.

None of this implies that there can't be a decoupling of the US-China relationship – both in real terms through trade flows and in financial terms through capital flows. In fact, I stressed precisely this concern in a book I published a few years ago on the perils of Sino-American codependency. With China reliant on the US consumer as a major source of external support for its export-led growth model, and the US dependent on China as its third-largest and fastest-growing export market (as well as the largest foreign buyer of Treasury securities), both countries needed and welcomed the other's support. But, as with human beings, conflict arises when one codependent partner changes the terms of the relationship, as China has done by shifting from export- to consumer-led growth. The current trade war is a classic example of the conflict phase of codependency.

There is a striking irony to a tariff war being instigated by the US, the world's largest deficit saver. In light of its ominous fiscal trajectory, America will be even more prone to large trade deficits in the years ahead. Closing off the China option through a bilateral decoupling will do nothing to reduce the overall size of the US trade gap. It will merely force a rearrangement of the pieces of America's multilateral trade deficit with its other trading partners.

That poses an even thornier political problem. The trade diversion arising from bilateral decoupling would mean that US sourcing would migrate from low-cost Chinese production platforms to a broad constellation of foreign producers. Whether that pushes trade to other Asian platforms or even "re-shores" it back to the US, as President Donald Trump has long insisted would happen, the bottom line is a likely shift to higher-cost production platforms. Ironically, that would be the functional equivalent of a tax hike on US companies, workers, and households. In the end, that underscores the potential for the most contentious decoupling of all in the years ahead – between America's politicians and its long-beleaguered middle class. ⓟ

Stephen S. Roach, a faculty member at Yale University and former Chairman of Morgan Stanley Asia, is the author of Unbalanced: The Codependency of America and China.

◢ PROTESTS AGAINST HUAWEI CFO MENG WANZHOU'S 2019 COURT APPEARANCE IN VANCOUVER.

Inequality in Cambridge and Chicago

ANGUS DEATON
2015 Nobel Laureate in Economics

Many people seem to be losing faith in capitalism, and with it, any faith they had in economists, who are seen as its apologists. The *New York Times* reporter Binyamin Appelbaum's new book, *The Economists' Hour*, raises many uncomfortable questions. Did economics take a wrong turn? Did those of us who do *not* subscribe to its Chicago School neoclassical variant nonetheless allow ourselves to be pushed too far in that direction? Would the world have been a better place if Cambridge economists had achieved more influence, and Chicago economists less? And, by Cambridge, I of course mean Cambridge, England.

WHEN I BECAME AN ECONOMIST IN Cambridge 50 years ago, economists and philosophers talked to one another, and welfare economics was taught and taken seriously. John Rawls's landmark 1971 work *A Theory of Justice* was much discussed, and Amartya Sen, Anthony Atkinson, and James Mirrlees, all then in Cambridge, thought about justice and its relationship with income inequality.

Sen, inspired by Kenneth Arrow's *Social Choice and Individual Values*, which he read as an undergraduate in Calcutta, wrote about social choice theory, relative and absolute poverty, and utilitarianism and its alternatives. Mirrlees solved a version of the question of how to reconcile a preference for equality with the need to respect incentives, and Atkinson showed how to integrate views about inequality with their measurement.

Meanwhile, in the United States, the Chicago School was following a different line. No one should doubt the intellectual contributions of Milton Friedman, George Stigler, James Buchanan, and Robert Lucas to economics and political economy, as well as those of Ronald Coase and Richard Posner to law and economics. Yet it is hard to imagine a body of work more antithetical to broad thinking about inequality and justice. Indeed, in the most extreme versions, money becomes the measure of wellbeing, and justice is nothing more than efficiency. When I came to the US in 1983 and was called out as "unprofessional" for thinking about inequality, I thought of my own reaction years earlier to reading Stigler's 1959 argument that "the professional study of economics makes one politically conservative." I had thought it was a typo; I had never met a conservative economist.

The influence of Chicago economics and of Friedman's own arguments remain extraordinarily wide. Friedman dismissed much of inequality as natural, reflecting the choices of people with heterogeneous tastes. He believed in equality of opportunity but stridently opposed the estate tax as "a bad tax" that "taxes virtue" and "encourages wasteful spending." More than 700 economists recently endorsed these claims, and today we hear the same arguments against a wealth tax. For Friedman, who

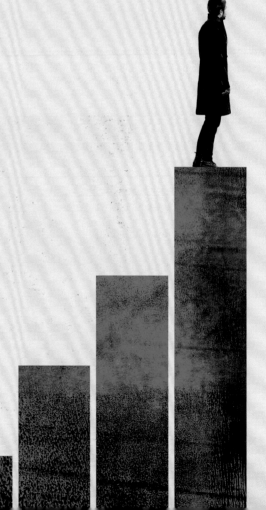

also favored tax competition between countries, efforts to limit inequality of outcomes would not only stifle freedom but would also result in more inequality. Free markets would produce both freedom and equality.

It doesn't seem to have worked out that way.

Instead, we got a world in which the Sackler family paid themselves more than $12 billion for igniting and promoting an opioid epidemic that has killed hundreds of thousands of Americans. Johnson and Johnson, the makers of Band-Aids and Baby Powder, grew opium poppies in Tasmania to fuel the epidemic while the US military was targeting the Taliban's opium supply in Afghanistan's Helmand Province. In 1839, the British sent gunboats to make China safe for British (and Indian) opium smugglers. We have private equity firms buying up ambulance services and staffing hospital emergency rooms with their own physicians so that they can charge "surprise" fees even to patients whose insurance covers that particular hospital.

This is exactly how we would expect unregulated markets to work: establish a local monopoly and charge a high price in the face of inelastic demand by unconscious (sometimes literally so) consumers. At least in retrospect, it is not surprising that free markets, or at least free markets where government allows rent seeking by the rich, produce not equality but an extractive elite. After all, this is not the first time that utopian rhetoric about freedom has produced an unjust social dystopia.

Appelbaum's best example is the achievement of which Friedman was most proud: the introduction of an all-volunteer military, which I suspect most economists still favor. But is it really a good idea to draw our military from those with less education and fewer opportunities? In 2014, only 7% of enlisted troops had a bachelor's degree, compared with 84% of officers.

Anne Case of Princeton University and I have been exploring widening inequalities between the less and well educated in the US. We have found a growing divergence in wages, labor-force participation, marriage, social isolation, pain, alcoholism, drug deaths, and suicides. And now the less educated are being asked to risk their

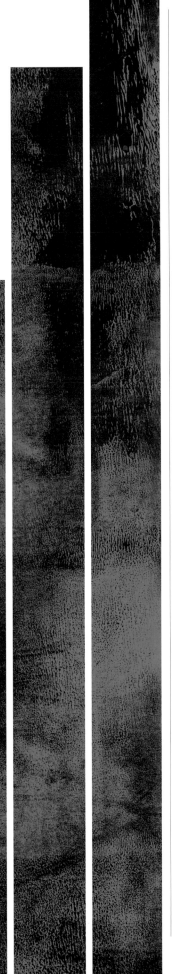

lives for an educated elite, who choose where, when, and whom to fight.

We have lost the social connectedness that came from all kinds of people serving together. Listen, for example, to the Nobel laureate economist Robert Solow describe his experience in the army as one of the best and most important periods in his life. If US President Donald Trump were to reject the 2020 election results, or refuse to leave the White House after being impeached and convicted, we may come to regret the social divisions that have given us an enlisted military selected from the places and people who most fervently support him.

Chicago economics gave us all a healthy respect for markets, but it also gave us too little regard for what markets cannot do, do badly, or should not be called upon to do at all. Philosophers have never accepted that money is the sole measure of good, and economists spend too little time reading and listening to them.

But change may be on the horizon. The Nobel laureate economist Peter Diamond was a longtime collaborator of Mirrlees, and his work with Emmanuel Saez is helping to shape plans by US Senator Elizabeth Warren, a leading candidate to challenge Trump in 2020, to re-institute high marginal tax rates on the rich. Whatever the outcome of the 2020 election, more attention to Cambridge economics might help restore faith, not only in capitalism, but also in economics itself. **PS**

Angus Deaton, *the 2015 Nobel laureate in economics, is Professor of Economics and International Affairs Emeritus at Princeton University's Woodrow Wilson School of Public and International Affairs.*

Europe's Hard Choices in 2020

ZAKI LAÏDI
Professor of International Relations at Sciences Po

For the first time since 1957, Europe finds itself in a situation where three major powers – the United States, China, and Russia – have an interest in weakening it. They may squeeze the European Union in very different ways, but they share an essential hostility to the EU's governance model.

THE EUROPEAN MODEL, AFTER ALL, is based on the principle of shared sovereignty among states in crucial areas such as market standards and trade. That liberal idea is antithetical to the American, Chinese, and Russian view of sovereignty, which places the prerogative of states above global rules and norms of behavior. Shared sovereignty is possible only among liberal states; unalloyed sovereignty is the preserve of populists and authoritarians.

But today's anti-EU hostility also owes something to Europe's undeniable economic weight in the world. Without the EU, the US under President Donald Trump would likely have succeeded already in forcing Germany and France to surrender to its trade demands. Were it on its own, France would not have been able to reject bilateral negotiations with the US over agricultural issues. The EU, as a "common front," works as a power multiplier for its constituent parts in all areas where sovereignty is shared.

China's view of Europe is not so different from Trump's. While the Chinese have taken advantage of the European single market by acquiring footholds in key EU countries, the last thing they want is for Europeans to share sovereignty in controlling foreign investment, such as through the new screening mechanism launched in April. China has been cultivating financial dependencies in the Balkans, knowing full well that if these countries become EU members, they will be subject to stronger transparency requirements.

China would much prefer the model underpinning the Belt and Road Initiative (BRI), its massive effort to build trade and transport infrastructure linking China with Africa and Europe. How China and participating countries finance BRI projects is notoriously opaque. In fact, more than half of all Chinese loans to developing countries are not even listed publicly.

Russia, too, resents European unity. Although some EU member states oppose continued sanctions against Russia, all have respected them. Still, Europe is hardly a monolithic bloc when it comes to Russia. Despite Europe's energy-independence objectives, Germany is cooperating with Russia in building the Nord Stream 2 gas pipeline. For a while, Germany also stood in the way ▶

Still, Europe is hardly a monolithic bloc when it comes to Russia."

of a firmer EU policy *vis-à-vis* China, owing to the German auto industry's reliance on the Chinese market. But Germany's position has changed since 2017, with its leaders finally taking stock of the risks posed by Chinese takeovers in sensitive industrial sectors.

The frequent claim that Europe is incapable of playing a global role is thus simply incorrect. Compared to a more isolated developed country like Japan, Europe is quite strong indeed. While Japan has been at the mercy of US tariffs on imported steel, the EU has retaliated in kind. And while Japan has had little choice but to accept a bilateral trade deal with the US ("in principle"), Europe has stonewalled the Trump administration's attempts to overhaul the US-EU trade arrangement.

To be sure, the EU is still a long way from achieving strategic and economic autonomy. But that does not mean it is incapable of doing so. Europe has many assets with which to defend multilateralism and international norms. Given its creativity and massive market, it could play a critical role in setting the standards for digitalization and artificial intelligence – both of which are at the heart of today's global economic battle. Lest one forget, it was Europe that took the first step in regulating the platform economy, through the General Data Protection Regulation, which has already set a new world standard.

But Europe still needs to develop its monetary, industrial, and military capacity. The EU must expand the international role of the euro so that it can serve as a safe asset and a standard currency for cross-border

trade. Internationalizing the euro will require a deep capital market, comparable to that of the US, and there is already a consensus among eurozone member states in favor of heading in this direction.

Establishing the euro as a safe asset – that is, making a Eurobond equivalent to a US Treasury bill – is more controversial. Germany is staunchly opposed to any proposal that implies risk-sharing across the eurozone. But if foreign investors are not confident that the European Central Bank will defend the value of the euro in any eurozone country, they will never see the single currency as a rival to the dollar.

On the second point, Europe needs to create its own industrial "champions." That will require deepening the internal market, which remains far too fragmented

(De)Reconstruction

with respect to services. It also may call for a reconsideration of EU competition rules. Following EU antitrust authorities' decision to block a number of large mergers in 2019 – not least that between Alstom and Siemens – there is a growing debate within Europe about how competition policies can be improved.

Finally, Europe desperately needs to build up its military capacity, to lend credibility to its exercise of commercial and soft power. For example, a new European protection force deployed in the Strait of Hormuz would signal to both the US and Iran that Europe can defend its own interests without having to take sides against its allies. The capacity to project power is a fundamental source of global clout.

Europe does not need a "grand strategy," which is a pompous term that fails to account for local and global constraints. Rather, it needs the determination and political will to develop new commercial, diplomatic, and military strategic assets. In a world of saber-rattling and muscle-flexing, effective modesty is preferable to vacuous ambition. ⚑

Zaki Laïdi is Professor of International Relations at Sciences Po.

Rediscovering Iran's Potential

JAVIER SOLANA
President of the Esade Center for Global Economy and Geopolitics

Almost a millennium ago, one of the most renowned Persians in history, Omar Khayyam, was born in the city of Nishapur in present-day Iran. In the West, Khayyam is known mainly as a poet, owing to the translation of his most important works into English in the nineteenth century. But, in his time, he forged his reputation mostly in mathematics and astronomy. In fact, the practice of representing the unknown in an equation with an x is thought to derive from Khayyam himself. He referred to unknowns as *shay* ("thing" in Arabic), a term that in old Spanish was transcribed as *xay*, from which supposedly emerged the now universally used *x*. ▶

MANKIND OWES INNUMERABLE advances to Persian thinkers, who for centuries distinguished themselves by their extraordinary scientific sophistication. Today, Iran ranks fifth in the world for the number of recent graduates in the STEM subjects (science, technology, engineering, and mathematics), behind only China, India, the United States, and Russia. In this regard, Iran is well ahead of technological powerhouses such as Japan – which has, moreover, a population that is around 50% larger.

Nevertheless, scientific progress can be a double-edged sword. That was true, for example, of Iran's clandestine nuclear program, which came to light in 2002. Although Iran's leaders insisted that the program's aims were peaceful and fully compatible with the Nuclear Non-Proliferation Treaty, the international community reacted with caution. Thus, as the European Union's high representative, I was tasked with reaching a diplomatic understanding with Iran, whose first negotiator was Hassan Rouhani, the national security adviser at the time. After many ups and downs, the circle finally closed in 2015, when the main global powers and Iran – where Rouhani had become president – reached a truly historic nuclear agreement: the Joint Comprehensive Plan of Action (JCPOA).

Diplomacy is never a bed of roses, and there are no shortcuts for those who practice it. Rouhani was indeed a tough negotiator, as I had expected, but I always appreciated his open and receptive approach. In 2013, after I had left active politics, Rouhani was kind enough to invite me to attend his first inauguration as president. After he explained his plans to me in detail during my visit, I had no doubt that Iran's new president was fully determined to leave behind the dark period of his predecessor, Mahmoud Ahmadinejad.

Trump the Destroyer

Building anything always requires tenacity and imagination, and Rouhani had both. Destroying something, on the other hand, requires little more than ambition. Unfortunately, US President Donald Trump has a surfeit of that. In May 2018, he withdrew the US from the JCPOA, and set out to crush the hard-won fruits of those slow and painstaking diplomatic efforts.

Despite Trump's incessant contradictions, we can deduce his current objective regarding Iran, because he has used a similar *modus operandi* in several other situations. His strategy of "maximum pressure" seeks to cause economic mayhem in Iran, so that its leaders will have no option but to negotiate again from a weaker position.

Yet, although US sanctions have seriously bruised Iran's economy, the Iranian regime is no closer to the abyss – or to negotiating again. Sticks won't work without carrots: Iran's leaders lack any incentive to negotiate if the Trump administration does not first offer some kind of concession.

In fact, the US economic offensive has strengthened Iran's less moderate political forces. The chief beneficiary has been the Islamic Revolutionary Guard Corps (IRGC), a semi-autonomous arm of the Iranian military that has protected the integrity of the regime since the 1979 Islamic Revolution.

The IRGC has recently shored up its domestic popularity by adopting a tone that is more nationalist than religious, and many Iranians consider the US designation of the group as a foreign terrorist organization to be a national affront. Moreover, by hampering global commerce with Iran, the US sanctions have helped to enrich the IRGC, which is filling the gaps left by foreign multinational firms and also controls the channels of contraband.

There is no doubt about the IRGC's highly problematic influence elsewhere in the Middle East. Its so-called Quds Force, under the command of the charismatic General Qassem Soleimani, is responsible for extraterritorial operations and has proxies in Iraq, Syria, Lebanon, and Yemen, among other countries.

In 2016, the IRGC reportedly established a "Shia Liberation Army" under the aegis of the Quds Force, to be composed largely of foreign combatants. Such activities badly damage Iran's international image. Approaching Iran's leaders would be much easier if they made it clear that they were content to head a conventional state, rather than an expansionist liberation movement.

At the same time, Iran's footprint in the Middle East would be much fainter had countries like the US, Israel, and Saudi Arabia not made so many unforced errors. These blunders, which range from the war in Iraq to the war in Yemen, have brought Iran significant geopolitical gains at a very low cost.

Ideally, the major regional powers would start to smooth over their differences by working to end the war in Yemen, where the bombing campaign instigated by Saudi Arabia's *de facto* leader, Crown Prince Mohammed bin Salman, has led to a humanitarian tragedy. The current fragility of the pro-Saudi coalition – in which the United Arab

To add to the complexity, electoral cycles in Iran and America are synchronized. The US presidential and congressional elections in November 2020 will be sandwiched between Iran's parliamentary election in February and its presidential contest, scheduled for 2021 (in which Rouhani will be ineligible, having completed his second consecutive term). This imminent electoral whirlwind makes it even harder for Iran to soften its stance: the regime's more conservative wing, which hopes to capitalize on US policy fluctuations at the polls, is putting heavy pressure on the moderates.

Victories for the extremes in both countries would likely deepen the unproductive mutual hostility that has marked US-Iranian relations for most of the past 40 years. But should more moderate voices prevail, there will still be a chance to unlock Iran's rich peaceful potential. After all, diplomacy has succeeded once in recent years. We shouldn't exclude the possibility that it might do so again. **PS**

Emirates has recently assumed a lower profile – could yet ease the path toward a negotiated solution.

Understanding Iran

Although there are plenty of reasons to mistrust Iran, no diplomatic initiative can succeed if the only item on the table is resentment. To avoid getting lost in a spiral of accusations, any diplomat worth their salt must be able to empathize with others, which is not the same as defending them.

In the case of Iran, that requires recognizing the factors that feed its leaders' sense of insecurity. We should not forget that Shia Muslims are a clear minority in the region, and that, unlike other religious groups, they have no nuclear weapons. Furthermore, America's deplorable record of changing foreign regimes in times of peace began in Iran, with the 1953 overthrow of Mohammad Mosaddegh, the democratically elected prime minister.

All of these factors are deeply embedded in Iran's popular consciousness and are reflected in the Islamic Republic's official narrative. Rouhani was nonetheless able to

> Even Iranian scientists engaged in incontrovertibly benign activities are feeling the effects of US sanctions."

overcome the rancor, together with the other JCPOA signatories. But, just when the clouds were beginning to clear, America has summoned a downpour. By withdrawing from the 2015 nuclear deal and imposing fresh extraterritorial sanctions on third countries, the Trump administration has presented governments and businesses around the world with an intolerable dilemma: either they lose access to the US financial system, or they again condemn Iran to sterile isolation.

The US-generated storm threatens to demolish all Western bridges with Iran, including in sectors, like science, that have clear liberal tendencies. Even Iranian scientists engaged in incontrovertibly benign activities are feeling the effects of US sanctions. As long as the US ultimatum lasts, Iran's enormous scientific potential – not only for generating knowledge, but also for promoting international cooperation – will remain unfulfilled. The same applies to the overall wellbeing of Iranians, who have long suffered the consequences of both domestic and international political outrages.

Javier Solana, a former EU High Representative for Foreign Affairs and Security Policy, Secretary-General of NATO, and Foreign Minister of Spain, is currently President of the Esade Center for Global Economy and Geopolitics and Distinguished Fellow at the Brookings Institution.

The End of Gandhi's India?

On October 2, the world marked the 150th anniversary of the birth of Mohandas Karamchand "Mahatma" Gandhi – the greatest Indian of modern times. In a *New York Times* op-ed for the occasion, Prime Minister Narendra Modi, the most powerful living Indian, duly praised his country's independence leader. Between recalling the admiration for Gandhi of Martin Luther King, Jr., Nelson Mandela, Albert Einstein, and others, Modi saw fit to tout his own government's commitment to sanitation and renewable energy. ▶

THAT IS A LOT OF GROUND TO COVER.
Yet for this reader, the commentary
was most striking in what it did
not say. There was not a word about
the cause for which Gandhi lived –
and sacrificed – his life: interfaith
harmony. From the 1890s, when
he was an organizer for a small
community of diaspora Indians in
South Africa, to his death in 1948, by
which time he was the acknowledged
"Father" of a nation of over 300
million people, Gandhi worked to
build unity and solidarity between
Hindus and Muslims. While in
South Africa, many of the meetings
he organized to protest against
discriminatory laws were held in
mosques. And when he returned to
India, he fasted and embarked on
several long pilgrimages to build
trust between Hindus and Muslims.

Gandhi had fought the British,
non-violently, for an independent
and united India. In the end, he
achieved independence but not
unity. When the British finally gave
up the subcontinent in August 1947,
they partitioned it. Pakistan was
explicitly created as a homeland for
Muslims. But, owing to Gandhi's
efforts, India itself was established
as a nondenominational state:
the new constitution forbade
discrimination on religious grounds;
the Muslims who remained were
to be treated as equal citizens.

For the first two decades after
independence, minority rights in
India were carefully safeguarded,
owing chiefly to the determination
of the country's first prime minister,
Jawaharlal Nehru, to prevent India
from becoming a Hindu Pakistan.
In more recent times, however, India's
large (and mostly poor) Muslim
minority has come under increasing
attack. This is partly because, after
Nehru's death, the ruling Congress
Party shunned progressive Muslim
voices in its efforts to cultivate the
ulema (Muslim clergy) for votes.
But it is also because the traditional
opposition party, Modi's Bharatiya
Janata Party (BJP), has emphatically
rejected Gandhi and Nehru's vision
of political and religious pluralism.

From the mid-1980s, the country
was riven by a series of communal
riots in which Hindu mobs taunted
their Muslim compatriots with the
slogan *Pakistan ya Babristan!* (Go to
Pakistan, or be sent to the graveyard!)
The bloodiest riot was in 2002,
in Gujarat, where Modi was then
serving as chief minister. The episode
badly tarred Modi's image, and even
resulted in his being barred from
entering the United States for a while.

But having rebranded himself as a
Vikas Purush (Man of Development)
and devised a platform promising
inclusive growth, Modi was able to
prevail in the 2014 general election.
That outcome led to another wave
of hate crimes against Muslims,
which Modi proved either unable
or unwilling to prevent. His first
term in office yielded nothing for the
economy, so he and the BJP contested
the 2019 elections on a platform of
jingoistic nationalism. Pakistan was
depicted as the "Enemy Without,"
and Indian Muslims and secular
liberals as the "Enemies Within."

▲ INDIA'S FIRST PRIME MINISTER,
JAWAHARLAL NEHRU.

▼ A SURVIVOR OF THE 2002 HINDU-
MUSLIM VIOLENCE IN AHMADABAD.

Notwithstanding Modi's public posturing in the pages of Western newspapers, he and his party remain committed to the idea of a Hindu *Rashtra*: a state run for and by Hindus. There is currently just one Muslim among the BJP's 300-odd members of the Lok Sabha (the lower house of India's parliament). Worse, senior BJP leaders routinely insult and intimidate Indian Muslims without provocation, demanding that they prove their "loyalty" to the Motherland.

It is no accident that Modi failed to mention Hindu-Muslim harmony even when praising Gandhi. His silence speaks for itself. Meanwhile, on October 1, Modi's right-hand man, Amit Shah, the home minister and current BJP president, offered his own implicit message to India's Muslims. "I today want to assure Hindu, Sikh, Jain, Buddhist, and Christian refugees, you will not be forced to leave India by the Centre," he said in a speech in Kolkata. "Don't believe rumors," he added. "We will bring a Citizenship Amendment Bill, which will ensure these people get Indian citizenship."

Notably absent in these remarks was any reassurance for Muslim refugees, including those from Bangladesh, whom Shah previously referred to as "termites." The purpose of his speech was clear: Indian Muslims should be careful what they say, or they could find themselves stripped of citizenship and deported.

As Gandhi's biographer – and as an Indian citizen who is committed to pluralism – I am deeply worried about the escalating demonization of my Muslim compatriots. The democratic, secular republic that Gandhi fought for is being transformed into a Hindu majoritarian state.

Yet as a historian, I have no illusions about what we are witnessing. India, once an exception, is now converging toward the South Asian norm. Sri Lanka and Myanmar are both Buddhist majoritarian states, and their minority populations – Tamil Hindus and Rohingya Muslims, respectively – are treated as second-class citizens (and much worse). Likewise, Bangladesh and Pakistan are Muslim majoritarian states, where Hindus (and sometimes Christians) have historically been persecuted.

As we enter a new decade, it is clear that Modi, Shah, and the BJP are committed to joining the club of ethno-nationalist states. In pursuit of that end, they have decisively repudiated the legacy of Gandhi and Nehru, inaugurating a dark new chapter in the history of modern India. **PS**

Ramachandra Guha *is a historian based in Bengaluru. His most recent book is* Gandhi: The Years that Changed the World, 1914–1948.

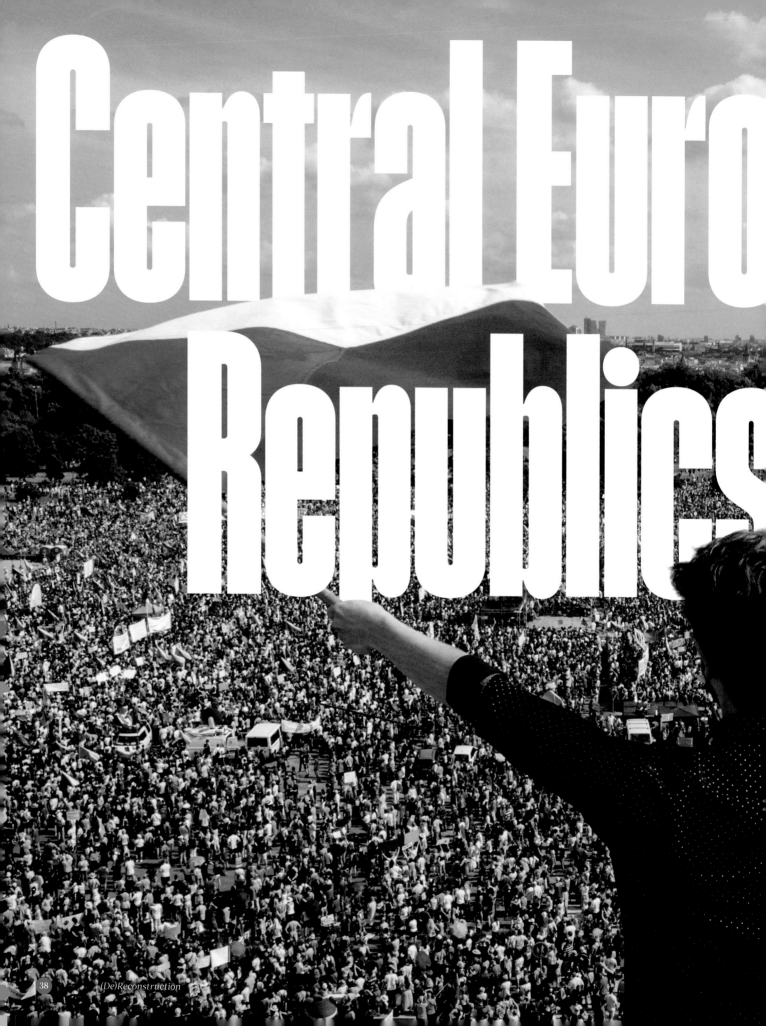

Central Euro Republics

(De)Reconstruction

e's of Fans

IVAN KRASTEV
*Chairman of the Center
for Liberal Strategies*

In Ferenc Karinthy's dystopian 1970 novel *Metropole*, a talented Hungarian linguist arrives at the airport in Budapest but then goes through the wrong gate, gets on the wrong plane, and lands in a city where no one can understand him, even though he speaks an impressive array of languages. Today, the unfortunate protagonist might find echoes of this tale in Central Europe, which has become one of the most politically confusing parts of the continent.

ALTHOUGH NUMEROUS OPINION POLLS INDICATE THAT the overwhelming majority of Poles, Hungarians, Czechs, and Slovaks value democracy and the rule of law, the region has not reversed the illiberal turn it took earlier this decade. In 2015, Adam Michnik, the Polish anti-communist dissident and editor of the liberal daily *Gazeta Wyborcza*, could say of the Law and Justice (PiS) party's parliamentary election victory that, "sometimes a beautiful woman loses her mind and goes to bed with a bastard." But PiS's repeat success in the October 2019 election suggests that the woman may have decided to marry him.

Why do voters who routinely profess a commitment to democracy also support political leaders who subvert it? And why do liberals' attempts to position themselves as guardians of democracy fail to bring them electoral success? These are precisely the questions that Milan Svolik, a political science professor at Yale, asked in the July 2019 issue of the *Journal of Democracy*.

Svolik's answer is straightforward: political polarization "undercut[s] the public's ability to curb the illiberal inclination of elected politicians." When voters have a choice between voting for the party they support in the knowledge that its leaders have violated democratic principles, or switching to an opposition party they detest in order to save democracy, most let their partisan instincts override their commitment to democratic norms.

As Svolik puts it, "voters are reluctant to punish politicians for disregarding democratic principles when doing so requires abandoning one's favorite party or policy." For many voters in these politically polarized times, the gravest threat to democracy is that their least-favored party wins an election.

Political polarization in Central Europe and elsewhere has turned the ideal "republic of citizens" into a "republic of fans." Whereas liberal citizens regard it as a sign of a higher loyalty to point out and correct the mistakes made by one's own party, the loyalty of fans is zealous, unthinking, and unswerving. The cheers of enthralled fans, with their critical faculties switched off, reflect and reinforce their sense of belonging, which is central to populists' understanding of politics as a game of loyalty.

In this kind of political world, US President Ronald Reagan's dictum "trust but verify" has given way to rowdy adulation: behold and adore. Those who refuse to applaud are traitors. Any statement of fact takes the form of a declaration of belonging. Any electoral defeat is unfair (or a conspiracy), and any criticism of one's own party is treason. Even when they are in government, populists prefer to view themselves as a persecuted minority. Their goal is to be viewed as underdogs who are entitled to act as roguishly relatable villains.

In a republic of fans, only moderate centrist voters, who do not identify strongly with any political party, can still put democratic principles above partisan loyalty. But centrists are out of fashion in today's highly polarized political environments, where the rejection of the other party defines how people vote, with whom they socialize, and how they view the world. In Central Europe these days, such voters are few and far between. Adapting a memorable line by Jim Hightower, a former Texas agriculture commissioner, to the region, "There's nothing in the middle of the road but a yellow stripe and dead armadillos."

Vilified by populists and anti-populists alike, many moderates prefer to move elsewhere. Thanks to the European Union's open borders, dissatisfied Central Europeans who want more democracy may find it easier to change their country of residence than their own government.

Svolik's research points to the critical problem facing liberal opposition

(De)Reconstruction

> Svolik's work also suggests that Central European liberals are doomed to fail when they attempt to reach out to culturally alienated voters by appealing to democratic principles."

parties in populist-governed Central Europe. As the recent municipal elections in Hungary and Poland's parliamentary election demonstrate, liberals are doing well in large urban centers and among young and better-educated voters, but they lose big in small towns and rural areas. Moreover, the distinct voting patterns and xenophobic attitudes are less the result of economic factors than of unfavorable demographic trends such as high emigration rates, a rapidly aging population, and an overhang of men of marriageable age.

In a similar vein, studies of political trends in the United States highlight the critical importance of the "density divide." Support for US President Donald Trump is highest in less densely populated regions in which white, native-born Americans constitute a clear majority. These voters generally are more socially conservative, do not favor diversity, are relatively disinclined to move elsewhere, and have no higher education.

Svolik's work also suggests that Central European liberals are doomed to fail when they attempt to reach out to culturally alienated voters by appealing to democratic principles. In fact, liberals who try to identify themselves with democracy, and define populist parties as its enemies, themselves contribute to the confrontational atmosphere that fuels the illiberal friends-versus-enemies narrative.

By making the defense of democracy their main political message, Central European liberals may manage to unify opposition forces, as happened recently in Hungary. But they will not succeed in reaching the supporters of populist parties. After all, voters living outside big cities expect liberals to defend not only democracy, but their interests, too. PS

▼ WOMEN IN TRADITIONAL HUNGARIAN DRESS CAST THEIR VOTES IN VERESEGYHAZ.

Ivan Krastev is Chairman of the Center for Liberal Strategies, Sofia, and the 2018–2019 Henry A. Kissinger Chair in Foreign Policy and International Relations at the John W. Kluge Center at the Library of Congress. He is the co-author (with Stephen Holmes) of The Light that Failed: A Reckoning.

Russia Is Not Putin

LYUBOV SOBOL
Russian opposition leader

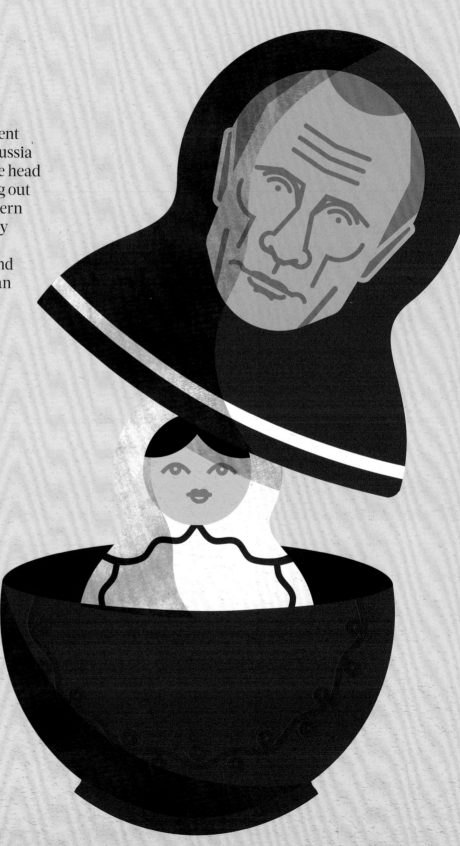

Russia is not synonymous with President Vladimir Putin, nor with his United Russia party, nor with Yevgeny Prigozhin, the head of a private military company carrying out the Kremlin's wishes in Syria and eastern Ukraine. Rather, Russia is embodied by its 146 million citizens, most of whom just want to live in a civilized world, and in a country where freedom and human rights are respected and upheld by credible independent institutions.

THE REAL VOICE OF RUSSIA OFTEN GOES UNHEARD, both within the country and abroad. Outside observers might think that the current government has the support of the population. But it isn't so. The mass protests in Moscow and other cities this past summer show that while formal power remains in the hands of Putin and his party, Russians are ready to assert their rights and demand democracy.

On the world stage, Putin falsely claims to wage his hybrid wars in our name. Yet there is never any formal declaration of war. And the Kremlin consistently denies that it is conducting military operations in Ukraine, because it knows that the Russian military's presence in Donbas and Crimea is illegal.

The Putin regime itself can be understood as a hybrid. Formally, Russia has a constitution that guarantees the rule of law, upholds the separation of powers, establishes an independent judiciary, and vests ultimate authority in the people. But, in reality, the Russian people have no influence over the authorities; all branches of government answer to Putin and his inner circle.

Likewise, while Russia holds formal elections, political representatives at the federal and regional levels are selected by the regime. And at the local level, decisions are made by regional governors, who are ultimately dependent on the central administration. Whenever necessary, the regime resorts to various methods to prevent genuine competition in elections: barring

opposition candidates from standing, blocking media coverage of opposition campaigns, and engaging in outright election fraud.

Consider the case of the anti-corruption lawyer Alexei Navalny. In March 2018, Navalny was the effective leader of Russia's democratic opposition, but he was prevented from running for president, and Putin easily clinched re-election in a field of Kremlin-picked candidates.

But in regional elections later that year, a massive protest vote signaled Russians' dissatisfaction with the regime. Many of United Russia's gubernatorial candidates – particularly those who had been pictured shaking Putin's hand before election day – were trounced, despite having had all of the administrative and propaganda resources of the state on their side. In Vladimir Oblast, the incumbent, Svetlana Orlova of United Russia, lost to Vladimir Sipyagin of the Liberal Democratic Party (LDPR). When asked by journalists why they had voted as they did, many people answered that they did not even know Sipyagin; they just wanted "anyone but Orlova."

In 2019, the authorities "corrected" their previous electoral "mistakes" by simply banning pro-democracy opposition candidates in particularly difficult regions. In some cases, even "pocket" opposition candidates (those from parties with seats in the Duma who run with the Kremlin's tacit imprimatur) were banned, including in remote regions such as Transbaikal. Nonetheless, in elections to the legislative assembly for Khabarovsk Territory, where pocket candidates were still allowed, the LDPR won out over United Russia.

I myself ran in elections to the Moscow City Duma, in which independent, democratically selected candidates were barred from running on the basis of absurd trumped-up charges, such as allegations of forging petition signatures to qualify for the ballot. In fact, we had significant support from our constituencies, and we appealed these illegal decisions in the courts. But, because the judiciary, too, is under the Kremlin's heel, justice was not served. Having been denied their choice of elected representatives, Muscovites by the tens of thousands took to the streets.

The authorities reacted to these protests with a wave of repression, detaining several thousand people and filing criminal charges against pro-democracy groups. Night searches were carried out in our houses, and dozens of people were jailed. The independent Anti-Corruption Foundation was declared to be a foreign agent, and our bank accounts were frozen. In late July, Navalny was poisoned with an unknown substance while under a 30-day administrative detention.

Putin was so scared of the Moscow elections that he deployed the full power of the courts, police, prosecutors, the Ministry of Justice, *Roskomnadzor* (the official censorship body), and other resources to derail the democratic opposition. The reason for this full-court press is obvious: an opposition victory in the capital would have destroyed the myth that Russians actually support Putin and his party, and that the democratic opposition represents just a small share of the population.

Putin has come to rely heavily on this myth, long a staple of state propaganda at home and abroad.

Free and fair elections in Moscow would have given the lie to his claim to legitimacy, and the other regions across Russia would have taken note of what was happening in the capital.

The Kremlin could not permit such a dangerous precedent. Putin wants the world to think that he represents the Russian people. But there can be no more compelling evidence that his power rests on a lie than his violent crackdown on Russians who are demanding that their representatives be allowed to put that power to the test in free and fair elections. ▮S

Lyubov Sobol is a lawyer with the Anti-Corruption Foundation and one of the leaders of the opposition movement in Moscow.

How to Make the Internet Safe for Democracy

FRANCIS FUKUYAMA
Senior Fellow at Stanford University

In October, a confrontation erupted between one of the leading Democratic candidates for the US presidency, Senator Elizabeth Warren, and Facebook CEO Mark Zuckerberg. Warren had called for a breakup of Facebook, and Zuckerberg said in an internal speech that this represented an "existential" threat to his company. Facebook was then criticized for running an ad by President Donald Trump's re-election campaign that carried a manifestly false claim charging former Vice President Joe Biden, another leading Democrat contender, with corruption. Warren trolled the company by placing her own deliberately false ad.

THIS DUSTUP REFLECTS THE ACUTE problems social media pose for American democracy – indeed, for all democracies. The Internet has in many respects displaced legacy media like newspapers and television as the leading source of information about public events, and the place where they are discussed. But social media have enormously greater power to amplify certain voices, and to be weaponized by forces hostile to democracy, from Russian trolls to American conspiracy theorists. This has led, in turn, to calls for the government to regulate Internet platforms in order to preserve democratic discourse itself.

But what forms of regulation are constitutional and feasible? The US Constitution's First Amendment contains very strong free-speech protections. While many conservatives have accused Facebook and Google of "censoring" voices on the right, the First Amendment applies only to *government* restrictions on speech; law and precedent protect the ability of private parties like the Internet platforms to moderate their own content. In addition, Section 230 of the 1996 Communications Decency Act exempts them from private liability that would otherwise deter them from curating content.

The US government, by contrast, faces strong restrictions on its ability to censor content on the Internet in the direct way that, say, China does. But the United States and other developed democracies have nonetheless regulated speech in less intrusive ways. This is particularly true with regard to legacy broadcast media, where governments have shaped public discourse through their ability to license broadcast channels, to prohibit certain forms of speech (like terrorist incitement or hard-core pornography), or to establish public broadcasters with a mandate to provide reliable and politically balanced information.

The original mandate of the Federal Communications Commission was not simply to regulate private broadcasters, but to support a broad "public interest." This evolved into the FCC's Fairness Doctrine, which enjoined TV and radio broadcasters to carry politically balanced coverage and opinion. The constitutionality of this intrusion into private speech was challenged in the 1969 case *Red*

> "The rise and fall of the Fairness Doctrine shows how hard it would be to create an Internet-age equivalent."

Lion Broadcasting Co. v. FCC, in which the Supreme Court upheld the Commission's authority to compel a radio station to carry replies to a conservative commentator. The justification for the decision was based on the scarcity of broadcast spectrum and the oligopolistic control over public discourse held by the three major TV networks at the time.

The *Red Lion* decision did not become settled law, however, as conservatives continued to contest the Fairness Doctrine. Republican presidents repeatedly vetoed Democratic attempts to turn it into a statute, and the FCC itself rescinded the doctrine in 1987 through an administrative decision.

The rise and fall of the Fairness Doctrine shows how hard it would be to create an Internet-age equivalent. There are many parallels between then and now, having to do with scale. Today, Facebook, Google, and Twitter host the vast majority of Internet speech, and are in the same oligopolistic position as the three big TV networks were in the 1960s. Yet it is impossible to imagine today's FCC articulating a modern equivalent of the Fairness Doctrine. Our politics are far more polarized; reaching agreement on what constitutes unacceptable speech (for example the various conspiracy theories offered up by Alex Jones, including that the 2012 school massacre in Newtown, Connecticut was a sham) would be impossible. A regulatory ▶

FACEBOOK CEO
MARK ZUCKERBERG.

approach to content moderation is therefore a dead-end, not in principle but as a matter of practice.

This is why we need to consider antitrust as an alternative to regulation. The right of private parties to self-regulate content has been jealously protected in the US; we don't complain that the *New York Times* refuses to publish Jones, because the newspaper market is decentralized and competitive. A decision by Facebook or YouTube not to carry him is much more consequential because of their monopolistic control over Internet discourse. Given the power a private company like Facebook wields, it will rarely be seen as legitimate for it to make such decisions.

On the other hand, we would be much less concerned with Facebook's content moderation decisions if it were simply one of several competitive Internet platforms with differing views on what constitutes acceptable speech. This points to the need for a massive rethinking of the foundations of antitrust law.

The framework under which regulators and judges today look at

antitrust was established during the 1970s and 1980s as a byproduct of the rise of the Chicago School of free-market economics. As chronicled in Binyamin Appelbaum's recent book *The Economists' Hour*, figures like George Stigler, Aaron Director, and Robert Bork launched a sustained critique of over-zealous antitrust enforcement. The major part of their case was economic: antitrust law was being used against companies that had grown large because they were innovative and efficient. They argued that the only legitimate measure of economic harm caused by large corporations was lower consumer welfare, as measured by prices or quality. And they believed that competition would ultimately discipline even the largest companies. For example, IBM's fortunes faded not because of government antitrust action, but because of the rise of the personal computer.

The Chicago School critique made a further argument, however: the original framers of the 1890 Sherman Antitrust Act were interested only in the economic impact of large scale, and not in the political effects of monopoly. With consumer welfare

Economists and legal scholars are beginning to recognize that consumers are hurt by things like lost privacy and foregone innovation..."

THE FACEBOOK PAGE OF INFOWARS FOUNDER ALEX JONES.

◣ PIZZAGATE CONSPIRACY
ADHERENTS DEMONSTRATE
AT THE WHITE HOUSE.

the only standard for bringing a government action, it was hard to make a case against companies like Google and Facebook that gave away their main products for free.

We are in the midst of a major rethinking of that inherited body of law in light of the changes wrought by digital technology. Economists and legal scholars are beginning to recognize that consumers are hurt by things like lost privacy and foregone innovation, as Facebook and Google sell users' data and buy up startups that might challenge them.

But the political harms caused by large scale are critical issues as well, and ought to be considered in antitrust enforcement. Social media have been weaponized to undermine democracy by deliberately accelerating the flow of bad information, conspiracy theories, and slander. Only the Internet platforms have the capacity to filter this garbage out of the system. But the government cannot delegate to a single private company (largely controlled by a single individual) the task of deciding what is acceptable political speech. We would worry much less about this problem if Facebook was part of a more decentralized, competitive platform ecosystem.

Remedies will be very difficult to implement: it is the nature of networks to reward scale, and it is not clear how a company like Facebook could be broken up.

But we need to recognize that while digital discourse must be curated by the private companies that host it, such power cannot be exercised safely unless it is dispersed in a competitive marketplace. ⌘

Francis Fukuyama is a senior fellow at Stanford University and Co-Director of the Project on Democracy and the Internet.

(De)Reconstruction

Big Tech's Will to Power

ROGER MCNAMEE
Co-Founder of Elevation Partners

Although we have only just begun to understand the harms caused by Internet platforms to public health, privacy, and competition, we will soon be confronting an even more fundamental threat from Big Tech. At a time when the institutions of liberal democracy are already weak, Google, Facebook, Amazon, and Microsoft are mounting a challenge to democratically elected governments by offering their own services as an alternative.

THIS REPRESENTS A SIGNIFICANT change from the past. As recently as 20 years ago, America's technology companies had little interaction with the federal government beyond paying taxes. Engineers created products that empowered customers, and the government cheered them on.

But after the terrorist attacks of September 11, 2001, the country's attitude toward surveillance changed. The US intelligence community collaborated with leading digital platforms – starting with Google – to gather massive stores of personal data that might be used to prevent future attacks. Moreover, beginning in 2008, Google, Facebook, and others became indispensable tools for politicians. The tech industry's cozy relationship with President Barack Obama's administration protected it from scrutiny while it perfected what Shoshana Zuboff of Harvard Business School calls "surveillance capitalism."

Whereas industrial capitalism deploys technology to manipulate the environment, surveillance capitalism manipulates human behavior. Its practitioners convert human experience into data, create digital voodoo dolls (dossiers) representing each individual, and then use those virtual representations to fashion and sell behavioral-prediction products.

These products have transformed marketing and advertising, by supplementing demographic targeting with specific predictions for every potential customer. And the leading surveillance capitalists – Google, Facebook, Amazon, and Microsoft – also use the data they collect to manipulate individual search results, limiting the choices available to consumers and increasing the likelihood that they will behave as predicted. As Zuboff argues, surveillance capitalism threatens both individual autonomy and the viability of open societies.

Moving Fast...

The first evidence that Internet platforms could have a real-world impact on entire countries – not just individuals – came in 2016, when online disinformation campaigns featured prominently in the United Kingdom's Brexit referendum and the US presidential election. Since then, Internet platforms have enabled election interference in many other countries and unwittingly played a role in genocide in Myanmar, terrorism in New Zealand, mass murders in the United States and Europe, and measles outbreaks in countries where the disease had previously been eliminated. They are now regularly used to spread disinformation, foment violent extremism, and polarize electorates.

I do not believe that Internet platforms intended to enable these harms. But their business models, algorithms, and internal cultures made such harms inevitable. As citizens, we all need to acknowledge that Internet platforms now have as much or more of an impact on our lives than our governments do. When Facebook prohibits images of breastfeeding, its users cannot appeal the decision, even if they live in a country with constitutional protections for speech. And when it changes its policies to permit false advertising in political campaigns, it is essentially inviting further attacks on our elections – and thus on democracy itself. ▶

Worse, open societies have yet to get a hold on the first wave of harm unleashed by the Internet platforms. The most thoughtful initiatives to date – the European Union's General Data Protection Regulation and California's Consumer Privacy Act – address only a subset of the problem. Policymakers are still in the early stages of understanding how surveillance capitalism works. There is not even a consensus that this new economic model poses a threat, much less a plan to neutralize its harmful effects.

Meanwhile, Google, Facebook, Amazon, and Microsoft have already moved on to the next stage. Having perfected surveillance capitalism, they are in a position to launch initiatives designed to displace services traditionally provided by government. They are not the first companies to do this, but their ambitions and the means at their disposal far exceed those of other corporate privateers, such as the for-profit prison industry.

Each leading platform company is driven by a clear goal. Some are explicit, as with Google's mission to "organize the world's information" and Facebook's desire to bring the

Whether by design or by accident, this business model could gradually displace personal choice, and replace local-level democracy with algorithms."

world together on a single network. Others can be inferred from behavior: Amazon clearly wants to be the backbone of the economy, and Microsoft the technology partner for businesses and governments. In each case, the unstated objective is control. Not satisfied with the benefits of surveillance capitalism, which today are constrained by the size of the market for advertising, the platform firms are moving aggressively – and defiantly, in some cases – into new markets.

… and Breaking Things

For example, Sidewalk Labs, a subsidiary of Google's parent company, Alphabet, offers to take over local government services in exchange for control of public data and decision-making power. Whether by design or by accident, this business model could gradually displace personal choice, and replace local-level democracy with algorithms.

Likewise, with the planned launch of its cryptocurrency Libra, Facebook is trying to compete with reserve currencies like the US dollar and the euro. Although Libra initially

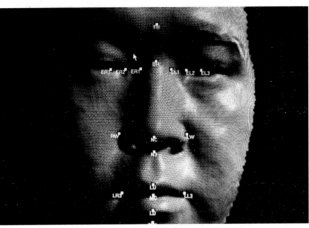

▲ TOP: MARK ZUCKERBERG
ANNOUNCING FACEBOOK'S PLANNED
CRYPTOCURRENCY, LIBRA.

▲ BOTTOM: BIOMETRIC FACIAL
RECOGNITION SOFTWARE.

had the support of many leading financial-services firms, its unveiling has triggered a global backlash, and many of those partners have dropped out. But regardless of what happens with Libra, Facebook will continue to play an outsize role in undermining democracy. Its open willingness to facilitate the dissemination of known falsehoods, along with its CEO's criticism of a leading Democratic presidential candidate (Elizabeth Warren), suggests that the company is not afraid to put its own interests before those of the country.

For its part, Amazon has moved aggressively into government contracting, providing a wide range of information services to federal and local agencies. It has offered facial-recognition products to law-enforcement agencies such as Immigrations and Customs Enforcement (ICE), even though the software currently suffers from implicit bias against people of color.

Amazon is also using its Ring line of smart doorbells to broker cooperation agreements with local police departments. When homeowners provide prior approval, law-enforcement officials can access Ring video feeds without a warrant. Civil-liberties advocates and experts are understandably concerned that when combined with facial-recognition technology, Ring doorbell networks will allow for new, potentially unconstitutional forms of surveillance. Journalists have also discovered that Amazon's Ring deals give the company undue leverage over how law-enforcement agencies communicate with the public.

Finally, Microsoft's new initiatives are less brazen, but not necessarily less problematic. For example, its work on artificial intelligence includes applications that would automate policing. As with facial recognition, early AI-based policing apps have been plagued by implicit bias. Regardless of whether this is a result of poor engineering or customer preferences, the fact is that no one has yet found a solution to the problem. Algorithmic bias has been found across a broad range of applications, such as in software that reviews resumes and mortgage applications.

Time Is Running Out

Over the past two decades, the leading Internet platforms have taken advantage of deregulation and legal loopholes to build globe-spanning businesses and amass enormous wealth. Success has bred arrogance, particularly at Facebook and Google, both of which have defied policymakers in contexts where other corporations have not. Both companies initially refused to send their CEOs to the first congressional hearings on election interference. And Facebook's Mark Zuckerberg has consistently avoided testifying before parliamentary committees in Canada and the UK, two of Facebook's largest markets. When Facebook and Google executives have appeared before oversight bodies, they have often been cagey and evasive.

These companies now dominate our lives, often in ways that we do not even realize. They are unelected and unaccountable, and they are replacing self-determination and democratic decision-making with algorithmic processes. Open societies cannot permit corporations to behave this way. As citizens, we must demand that our governments bring them to heel while they still have the power to do so. PS

Roger McNamee is a co-founder of Elevation Partners and an early investor in Facebook, Google, and Amazon.

1011

0110

1011

1100

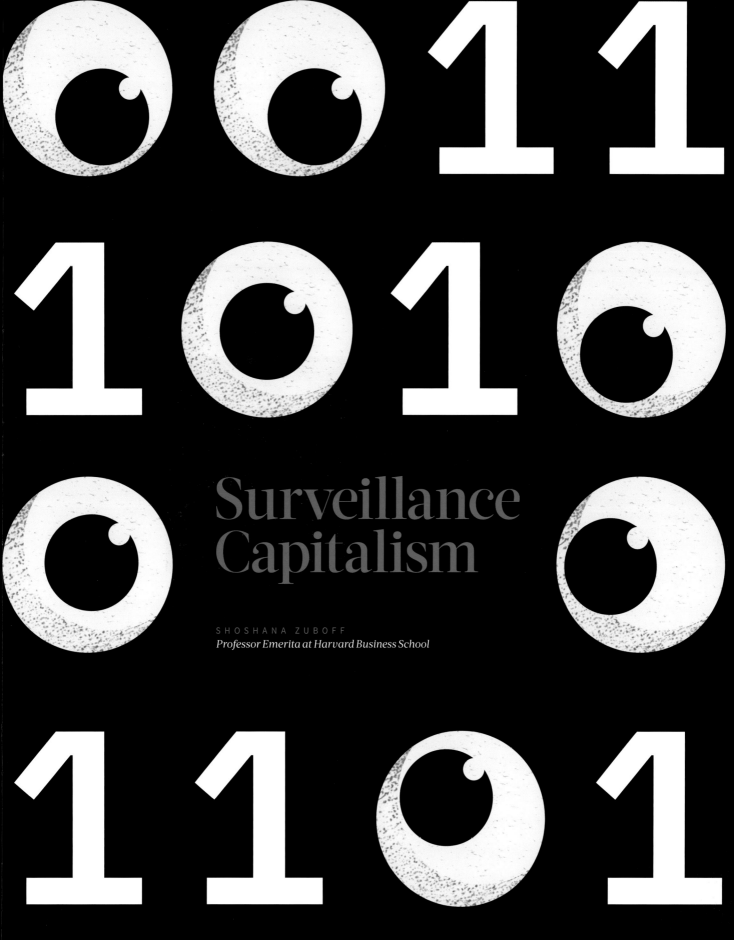

Surveillance Capitalism

SHOSHANA ZUBOFF
Professor Emerita at Harvard Business School

As we enter a new decade, we are also entering a new era of political economy. Over the centuries, capitalism has evolved through a number of stages, from industrial to managerial to financial capitalism. Now we are entering the age of "surveillance capitalism."

UNDER SURVEILLANCE CAPITALISM, people's lived experiences are unilaterally claimed by private companies and translated into proprietary data flows. Some of these data are used to improve products and services. The rest are considered a "behavioral surplus" and valued for their rich predictive signals. These predictive data are shipped to new-age factories of machine intelligence where they are computed into highly profitable prediction products that anticipate your current and future choices. Prediction products are then traded in what I call "behavioral futures markets," where surveillance capitalists sell certainty to their business customers. Google's "clickthrough rate" was the first globally successful prediction product, and its ad markets were the first to trade in human futures. Already, surveillance capitalists

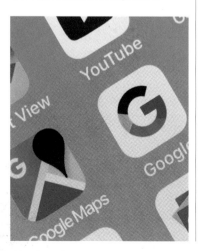

have grown immensely wealthy from these trading operations, and ever more companies across nearly every economic sector have shown an eagerness to lay bets on our future behavior.

The competitive dynamics of these new markets reveal surveillance capitalism's economic imperatives. First, machine intelligence demands a lot of data: economies of scale. Second, the best predictions also require varieties of data: economies of scope. This drove the extension of surplus capture beyond likes and clicks into the offline world: your jogging gait and pace; your breakfast conversation; your hunt for a parking space; your face, voice, personality, and emotions. In a third phase of competitive intensity, surveillance capitalists discovered that the most predictive data come from intervening in human action to coax, tune, herd, and modify behavior in the direction of guaranteed outcomes. This shift from knowledge to power transforms technology from a means of production to a global means of behavioral modification in order to achieve "economies of action."

I call this power to shape human behavior remotely and at scale toward others' ends "instrumentarian power," because it works entirely through the medium of digital instrumentation. Instrumentarian power will not threaten you with terror or murder.

POKÉMON GO PLAYERS
IN HONG KONG.

KARL MARX.

GOOGLE'S PRODUCT
ECOSYSTEM.

No soldiers will appear to drag you to the gulag or the camp. This new species of power works remotely, engineering subliminal cues, social comparison dynamics, rewards and punishments, and varieties of enforcers to shape behavior that aligns with its commercial interests.

Economies of action have been a focal point of experimentation. Facebook's "massive-scale contagion experiments" discovered how to engineer subliminal cues and social comparison dynamics on Facebook pages to change users' real-world behavior and emotions, while steadfastly bypassing user awareness. The Google-developed augmented-reality game *Pokémon Go* drove experimentation to a new level. Those participating in the *Pokémon Go* craze a few years ago were not just playing a smartphone game. In fact, the rewards and

Surveillance capitalism dismantles the early digital dream, which envisioned the Internet as a liberating, democratizing force."

punishments of gamification were used to herd people to restaurants, bars, fast-food outlets, and shops that had paid for guaranteed "foot traffic."

Just as industrial capitalism continuously intensified the means of production, surveillance capitalism is intensifying the means of behavioral modification. Surveillance capitalism dismantles the early digital dream, which envisioned the Internet as a liberating, democratizing force. One should no longer harbor any illusions that networks are inherently moral or that "connection" is intrinsically social, inclusive, and democratic. On the contrary, digital connection is now merely a means to someone else's commercial end. Surveillance capitalism is parasitic to the core, reprising Karl Marx's depiction of capitalism as a vampire that feeds on labor, ▶

only now labor has been replaced by private human experience.

Surveillance capitalism has been embraced by Facebook, Microsoft, Amazon, and many others, but it was first perfected by Google (now Alphabet), just as managerial capitalism was perfected by General Motors a century ago. As the pioneer, Google rapidly colonized the unmapped spaces of the unregulated Internet, where it thrived like an invasive species in an environment free of natural predators. It developed its business model at breakneck speed, far outpacing public institutions' or users' ability to follow it. But it also benefited from historical events. After the attacks of September 11, 2001, the US national-security apparatus was inclined to nurture, mimic, shelter, and appropriate, rather than regulate, surveillance capitalism's emergent capabilities.

Surveillance capitalists quickly realized that they could do anything they wanted, so that's what they did. While paying lip service to the emancipatory power of technology, the real action – the relentless secret extraction of private experience as free raw material for production and sales – was hidden offstage. Emboldened by vast and growing revenue streams and a wild, uncontested theater of operation, they were also protected by the inherent illegibility of automated processes. People simply didn't realize what was happening, and how the new economic logic really worked.

Having started with the major Internet companies, the mechanisms and economic imperatives of surveillance capitalism have become the default model for Internet-based businesses generally. Moreover, today's prediction products extend far beyond targeted online ads to many other sectors, including insurance, retail, finance, health, education, and an ever-widening range of goods and services.

These goods and services are not made for constructive producer-consumer reciprocities. Rather than being the objects of a traditional value exchange, they are the "hooks" that lure users into extractive arrangements, where their personal experiences can be harvested and packaged to serve others' ends.

A digital-age truism holds that, "If it's free, you are the product." But that is not right: you are the raw material in a much larger extraction process.

This implies a Faustian compact. We have all accepted that the Internet is now essential for social and economic participation. Yet to reap its benefits, we must subject ourselves to surveillance-capitalist exploitation. Because we are so dependent on the digital world, we have inured ourselves to the realities of being tracked, parsed, mined, and manipulated. We rationalize ("I have nothing to hide") or simply submit to the loss of privacy and agency, without realizing that a fundamentally illegitimate choice is being imposed on us.

How did it come to this? One of the most important features of surveillance capitalism is that it is unprecedented. By definition, unprecedented developments are initially unrecognizable. When we encounter something new, we try to understand it by placing it in the context of familiar categories. For example, when the first automobiles appeared, many relied on the term "horseless carriage" to make sense of the new technology.

When we interpret an unprecedented development in the present as a mere extension of the past, we risk normalizing the abnormal. This can be a dangerous error. When indigenous people on the pre-Columbian Caribbean islands first encountered armored Spanish soldiers marching onto their shores, they assumed that they were being visited by gods and sowed the seeds of their own destruction by welcoming the newcomers with exquisite hospitality.

Because it is unprecedented, surveillance capitalism exceeds the scope of our existing economic concepts. For example, we reach for words like "monopoly" and "privacy" when objecting to surveillance-capitalist practices. But while these terms certainly apply, they do not capture the essence of the new operations. Surveillance capitalism is not just about corporate governance or market power; it is about an entirely new logic of accumulation, one with its own original mechanisms, methods, imperatives, and markets. The consequences reach beyond

One of the most important features of surveillance capitalism is that it is unprecedented."

▼ DEMONSTRATORS PROTEST THE INFILTRATION AND MONITORING OF LOCAL MUSLIMS AND MUSLIM COMMUNITY ORGANIZATIONS.

▲ CAMBRIDGE ANALYTICA'S
FORMER LONDON OFFICES.

the conventional territory of the private firm and undermine democracy from above and below. From above, surveillance capitalism operates through unprecedented asymmetries of knowledge and power, increasing rather than diminishing social inequality. From below, surveillance capitalism's imperatives take aim at human autonomy, individual sovereignty, and agency – capabilities without which democracy is unimaginable.

Although surveillance capitalism is an entirely new force in economic history, we have already seen enough to know that it relies on flagrant contempt for the social norms and rights that are essential to a properly functioning democratic society. Just as industrial civilization flourished at the expense of nature, surveillance capitalism thrives at the expense of human nature.

We are now confronting the legacy of industrial capitalism in the global fight against catastrophic climate change. By giving free rein to surveillance capitalism, what will our own legacy be? **PS**

Shoshana Zuboff is Professor Emerita of Business Administration at Harvard Business School and the author of The Age of Surveillance Capitalism.

Protecting Competition in a Digital World

ANDREAS MUNDT
President of the
Bundeskartellamt

Digital technology continues to transform much of the global economy. The combination of Big Data, increases in computing power, and cloud-based systems has generated new services, and is rapidly changing existing industries. Platforms connecting different user groups have brought online search, social media, and e-commerce to consumers around the world. Owing to their reach, scale, and enormous growth, some of these platforms have become digital gatekeepers for the services they offer, and this has afforded them exclusive access to certain user groups. The payoffs from such practices are clear: the five largest companies in the world by market value – Microsoft, Amazon, Apple, Alphabet (Google) and Facebook – are all digital firms.

COMPETITION LAW ENTRUSTS antitrust authorities with the task of keeping markets open to competition. It seeks to limit the economic power of individual companies in order to ensure choice for consumers. If a dominant company acts as a digital gatekeeper and abuses its power, competition authorities should intervene to ensure contestability and protect consumers.

But how can competition authorities fulfill their proper function when digitalization is progressing so fast? First, we need to understand how the digital world works. The links between Big Data, privacy, and competition are becoming more apparent by the day. Because gathering, processing, and monetizing data is key to the digital economy, the new business models are strongly data-driven. Personal data play a major role in the delivery of services such as search engines, social networks, or those offered by "smart home" devices. As such, it has significant economic and competitive value.

There is no such thing as a free lunch, even in the digital age. Access to personal data is highly valuable for many companies, and is one of the key factors contributing to market power in data-driven economic sectors. How companies collect and process personal data is becoming increasingly relevant to their competitiveness and market performance. It is thus essential for competition authorities to assess the data-processing activities of dominant companies in these markets. And in this context, it is particularly important to account for potential overlaps with other areas of policy and law, not least consumer protection and privacy law.

> "Facebook's access to these data sources contributes substantially to its market power."

At the beginning of 2019, the Bundeskartellamt (Germany's competition authority) introduced far-reaching restrictions on how Facebook can process German user data. Under Facebook's terms and conditions, use of the social network requires one to agree to allow the company to collect one's data even beyond the Facebook website. Data from one's activities anywhere on the Internet or through smartphone apps can be assigned to one's internal profile with the company. And Facebook's access to these data sources contributes substantially to its market power.

The Bundeskartellamt's goal was to ensure that Facebook can no longer force its users to agree to the near-unrestricted collection and assignment of non-Facebook data. But Facebook appealed our decision, and the Düsseldorf Higher Regional Court suspended the new rules in a preliminary assessment, taking a different view of the key legal issues. Yet, given the importance of ensuring competition in the future digital economy, the Bundeskartellamt has appealed to the German Federal Court of Justice for further clarification.

In recent years, the Bundeskartellamt has dealt with several other digital cases, ranging from mergers to vertical agreements, and these have increased our awareness of new and emerging business models, and of potential areas for cooperation. One issue that we are focusing on is the role of hybrid platforms in e-commerce. Platforms such as Amazon enable third-party sellers to reach potential customers with their products and services. But these platforms also offer products and services of their own, which means they are providing their infrastructure to third parties that are also their competitors. Given the increasing market power of some of these hybrid platforms, the potential for conflicts of interest and abusive business practices is obvious.

Fortunately, the Bundeskartellamt recently secured far-reaching improvements for sellers active on Amazon marketplaces worldwide. In response to our competition concerns, Amazon has amended its terms to address many of the complaints that we have received from sellers. Among the issues addressed were Amazon's unilateral exclusion of liability, the termination and blocking of sellers' accounts, the court of jurisdiction in case of a dispute, and Amazon's handling of product information. Amazon's amendments were sufficient to allow us to terminate our proceedings against the company. But in a parallel case, the European Commission is now investigating Amazon's collection and use of transaction data.

As we've seen, the digital economy raises many new issues with respect to competition law and related policy areas. For our part, we are approaching these challenges with a solid economic and legal background, as outlined in reports such as "Competition Law and Data," which we co-authored with the French competition authority (L'Autorité de la Concurrence). With the experience we have gained from cases like those mentioned above, we are trying to give companies indications of what is and is not allowed under competition law.

Moreover, in 2017, the Bundestag amended the German Competition Act to clarify several important questions regarding the digital economy. And this fall, the German

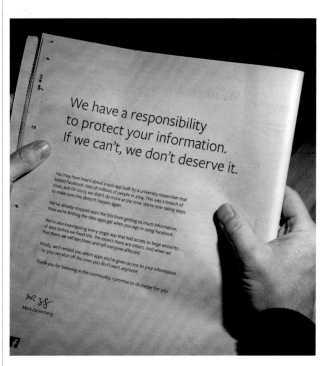

▲ FACEBOOK'S FULL-PAGE APOLOGY FOR MISHANDLING DATA.

◀ AN AMAZON FULFILLMENT CENTER IN THE UK.

Federal Ministry for Economic Affairs and Energy suggested further amendments that would make it easier to act against possible abuses by dominant digital platforms.

Consumer welfare, consumer choice, and the freedom to compete are intertwined. The Bundeskartellamt will continue to follow developments in the digital economy and enforce competition law, so that we can keep these markets open and free from abuse by the new gatekeepers. ▌S

Andreas Mundt is President of the Bundeskartellamt, Germany's competition authority.

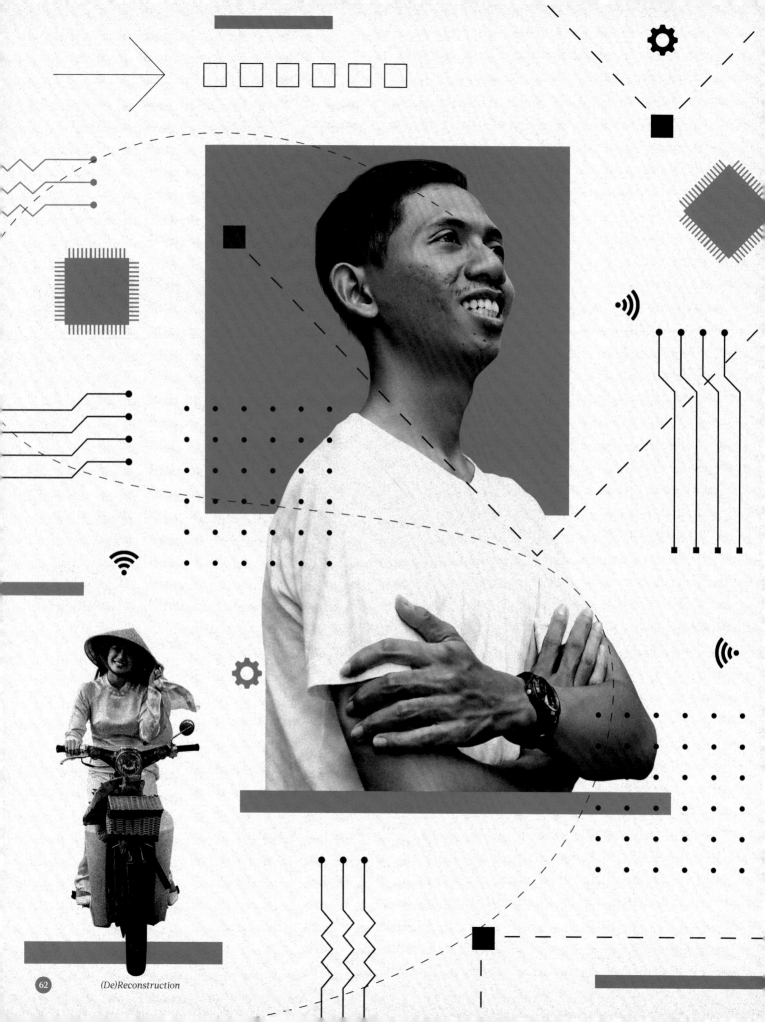

(De)Reconstruction

Developing Countries Must Seize the Tech Frontier

SRI MULYANI INDRAWATI
Finance Minister of Indonesia

Rapid technological transformation will be a key feature of the economy well into the future. At the national, regional, and global level, frontier technologies are offering promising new opportunities, but are also introducing new policy challenges.

THE MARCH OF TECHNOLOGICAL innovation has long boosted economic performance, improved efficiency, accelerated the pace of globalization, and transformed human society in the process. But as the defining issue of our time, the digital revolution demands renewed policy cooperation at all levels of governance. After all, the latest wave of technological change is especially broad, and it is coming fast. It is fundamentally altering how goods, services, and ideas are exchanged. And as rapidly declining costs make digital technologies even more affordable and accessible, they will continue to transform people's lives and livelihoods.

And yet, there is a danger that these gains will not reach the world's poorest people. An estimated three billion people could still lack Internet access by 2023, and many more will have little or no opportunity to reap the benefits of digital technologies. That means there can be no delay in addressing the problem of digital exclusion.

Fortunately, the Pathways for Prosperity Commission on Technology and Inclusive Development, which I co-chair with Melinda Gates, has shown that developing countries can still harness the new wave of frontier technologies for the benefit of all. Digital technologies have unlocked new routes to prosperity through agriculture, manufacturing, trade in services, the linking of informal and formal sectors, and domestic interconnectivity. Low- and middle-income countries around the world now have an opportunity to build new industries, deliver better services, and improve peoples' lives.

But digital technologies can also entrench existing forms of exclusion, disrupt livelihoods, and provide new tools for the powerful to abuse and exploit the weak. Developing countries, in particular, are starting from a difficult position, because they are already grappling with the challenges of low human capital, ineffective institutions, and a difficult business environment. Still, policymakers must not allow themselves to be paralyzed in the face of change. Rather than becoming passive observers of the tech revolution, they must take control of their countries' economic futures. ▶

3bn

AN ESTIMATED THREE BILLION PEOPLE COULD STILL LACK INTERNET ACCESS BY 2023.

(De)Reconstruction

> For its part, Indonesia recognizes the need for policies to manage the new digital economy."

All developing countries and emerging economies should be able to capture at least some of the new opportunities on offer. As the Commission has shown, governments have several policy options for achieving more inclusive growth. But technology alone will not guarantee success. Policymakers must also account for local contexts and conditions, so that they can create social, political, and economic ecosystems in which technology creates jobs and drives inclusive growth.

To compete globally, all countries will need to prepare themselves for new and upcoming technologies, by maximizing inclusiveness and guiding markets toward the right types of innovation. Governments should start by recognizing that the challenge is not just about "digital policy." Rather, it calls for a "whole-of-economy" – indeed, a "most-of-society" – approach. And because inclusion is the key to success, support for marginalized groups will need to be built into the policy process from the outset.

To that end, national governments should start planning for digital readiness in four areas: infrastructure, human capital, policy and regulation, and finance. These are the technical pillars of the future economy.

At the same time, regional-level policymakers – particularly in the Asia-Pacific region – need to start building momentum on policy cooperation, which will be necessary for harnessing frontier technologies for the greater good. Likewise, at the global level, cross-border issues associated with frontier technologies will need to be addressed multilaterally.

That means multilateral organizations themselves should be developing an antenna for identifying new technological and development challenges. It is already clear that more must be done to mitigate technological disruptions to employment, boost investment in human capital, and ensure fair taxation in the new digital economy.

We should not underestimate the power of multilateralism. For decades, countries have been coming together in global fora to safeguard public goods and pursue collective prosperity. Nonetheless, the existing architecture for multilateralism will need to be adapted to reflect changing needs. To capture the benefits of the Fourth Industrial Revolution, we also will need to strengthen public-private partnerships and make our economies more efficient and flexible. With the world's population projected to reach ten billion by mid-century, global governance will become even more complex than it is today.

For its part, Indonesia recognizes the need for policies to manage the new digital economy. In addition to addressing the impact of technological disruption and ensuring fair taxation, the key will be to put people at the center of the agenda. Beyond furnishing workers with the right skills, we must create a digital world where all people have a voice, and where those who are not benefiting from change have the support they need.

As is usually the case, the challenge we face is also an opportunity. Digital and frontier technologies have enormous potential to improve government administration and the delivery of public services. It is time for a new kind of conversation, one that involves governments, business leaders, innovators, civil-society organizations, and citizens alike. For developing countries, the task is clear: we must ride the wave of technological change, rather than wait for it to crash down on us. PS

A WORKER AT A SAMSUNG FACTORY IN CIKARANG, INDONESIA.

Sri Mulyani Indrawati is Finance Minister of Indonesia and former Chair of the World Bank Group's Development Committee.

A Fair Assessment

(De)Reconstruction

SHANG-JIN WEI
Professor of Finance and Economics at Columbia Business School

XINDING YU
Associate Professor of Economics at the University of International Business and Economics in Beijing

# of China's IP Protection

As 2020 approaches, US tariffs on Chinese goods have reached levels not seen since the US Smoot–Hawley Tariff Act of 1930, which played a key role in exacerbating the Great Depression. A key complaint of US President Donald Trump is China's failure to respect intellectual-property rights. Trump and his trade advisers regularly accuse China of stealing US inventions, designs, and other forms of IP without compensation, and many in the media repeat these allegations as a matter of course.

IT USED TO BE THAT ONE COULD WALK down the street in Vietnam, India, or Mexico and easily find pirated foreign movies and music on DVDs and CDs. Now that everything is digital, pirating has become less visible to tourists, even though it is probably no less rampant than before. In any case, IP protections are weaker in developing countries than in rich ones. The question, then, is whether China's record on IP is better or worse than what one would expect for its income level.

For systematic data on such questions, we examine countries' outbound royalty and license fee payments to foreign patent, copyright, and other IP holders, which is included in the balance-of-payments statistics compiled by the International Monetary Fund. These data reveal that a country's income level and IP payments are tightly linked, with a clear positive linear relationship (when both are measured in logarithm). As the graph shows, a 1% increase in *per capita* income is associated with a 1.85% increase in *per capita* IP payments, on average. The implication is that as a country grows richer – and as its economy becomes more technologically sophisticated and capital-intensive – its IP-protection regime tends to strengthen. (Recall that the United States was accused of violating British IP in the nineteenth century.)

If Chinese firms were systematically using foreign IP without compensation to a greater extent than other countries at a comparable income level, China's IP payments would be low for its income level. Yet when we created a time series for China's *per capita* IP payments between 1997 and 2017 (the red line in the graph), we found that this was

not the case. Before China joined the World Trade Organization in December 2001, its IP payments were below the international average for countries at a comparable income level. But in every year since its accession to the WTO, its IP payments have exceeded that average.

China's rapidly increasing IP payments have tracked its overall growth rate. In 2000, the last year before it joined the WTO, its total IP payments to foreigners were just $1.3 billion; by 2017, they had grown to $28.7 billion, implying a 20% average annual growth rate. For comparison, the median annual growth rate of IP payments across all countries during the same period was just 9.5%. China's IP payments have been growing at a significantly faster annual rate than that of France (7.9%), South Korea (6.5%), and Mexico

$1.3bn

CHINA'S IP PAYMENTS
TO FOREIGNERS IN 2000.

$28.7bn

CHINA'S IP PAYMENTS
TO FOREIGNERS IN 2017.

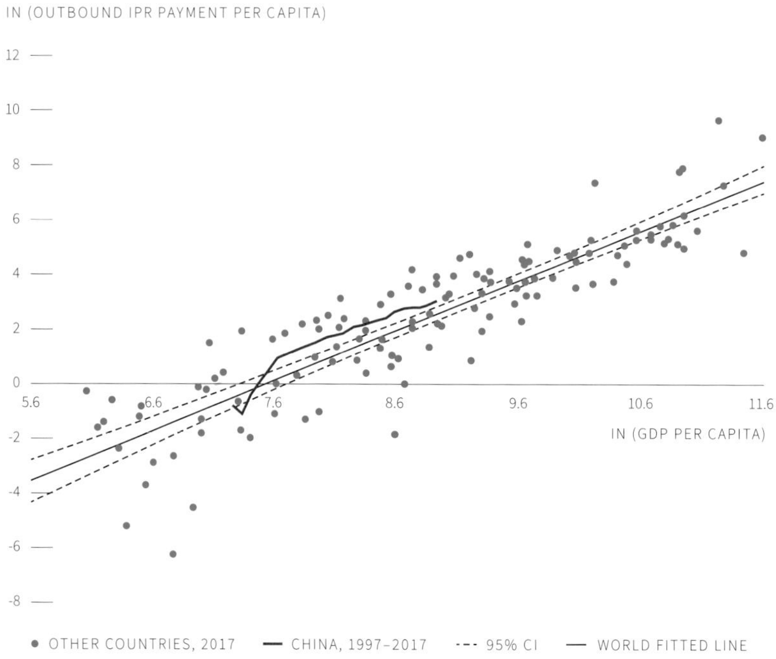

LN (OUTBOUND IPR PAYMENT PER CAPITA)

LN (GDP PER CAPITA)

● OTHER COUNTRIES, 2017 — CHINA, 1997–2017 --- 95% CI — WORLD FITTED LINE

▲ NIO ES8 ELECTRIC
VEHICLE ASSEMBLY LINE.

▲ HUAWEI EXPERIENCE STORE
PLUS OPENS IN XI'AN.

(-1.9%). India, with a population comparable in size to China's, has experienced a comparable rate of growth in IP payments; but its total IP payments, at $6.5 billion in 2017, were just 22% of the Chinese level.

Another way to gauge the effectiveness of Chinese IP protections is to look at where multinational firms locate their operations. Multinationals are not stupid. They are not inclined to enter markets where their property will be expropriated on a massive scale. In 2018, with the trade war already well underway, China was the top destination for foreign direct investment among all developing countries (as was the case in each of the previous ten years). In fact, among *all* countries, only the US attracted more FDI.

Reasonable people can draw different conclusions from these facts. On one hand, one could say that, compared to the US and other high-income countries, China is not doing enough to protect IP. Its IP regime could certainly be made stronger, and its *per capita* IP payments could be increased. But one could also say that China is doing exactly what is expected for a country at its income level. Indeed, its IP payments have long exceeded the international average. And as it becomes richer, the record suggests that its IP regime will grow stronger.

A final question is whether an agreement can be reached between China and other countries over IP. One key factor will be the pace of innovation within China. Chinese firms have made massive investments in research and development, and they are quickly increasing their own innovative output. The number of patents registered by Chinese firms is growing exponentially. Even if one does not trust official Chinese figures, a similar trend can be found in US patents granted to Chinese companies.

The accelerating pace of innovation within China should improve the prospects for cooperation on this issue. Whereas stronger IP rights used to mean higher rents for foreign firms, now those same protections will benefit Chinese firms, too.

China's IP regime is far from perfect. But the available evidence casts serious doubt on the claim that IP expropriation is unusually rampant there. Once the US can put the problem in proper perspective, greater cooperation with China in this area will look more promising. That, in the end, will benefit both sides far more than a tit-for-tat escalation of tariffs. **PS**

Shang-Jin Wei, a former chief economist at the Asian Development Bank, is Professor of Finance and Economics at Columbia Business School and Columbia University's School of International and Public Affairs.

Xinding Yu is Associate Professor of Economics at the University of International Business and Economics in Beijing.

Featuring exclusive content from **Asian Journal of Middle Eastern and Islamic Studies, Maritime Policy & Management, Social Sciences in China** and **Journal of Contemporary East Asia Studies** on the challenges, opportunities and impacts of the Belt and Road Initiative.

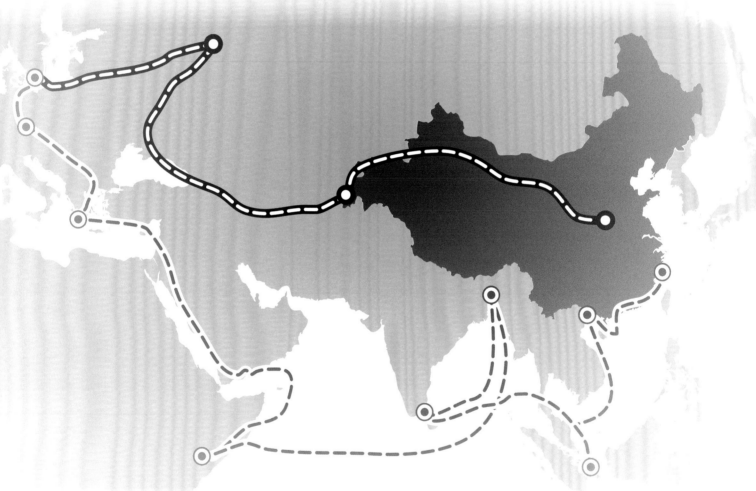

One Belt One Road Initiative

Browse free access articles here

http://bit.ly/OBOR-2019

Bring all of Project Syndicate's insightful content to your institution.

Access the insights of leading thinkers on the latest economic, geopolitical, and technology issues shaping your industry. Group subscriptions are available at advantageous rates for companies, organizations, or academic institutions.

Contact us at **subscriptions@project-syndicate.org** to learn more about group subscriptions or set yours up today.

Peace Through

MOON JAE-IN
President of the Republic of Korea

Peace is not a state of tranquility. Peace can come about only through dialogue and numerous meetings, by taking bold actions that make the impossible possible, and by persistently looking for reasons why it is preferable. ▶

(De)Reconstruction

Myriad Acts

I LIKE FORESTS. IF YOU TAKE A CLOSE look, you will discover that they are constantly on the move. Leaves conduct photosynthesis, ants march in single file transporting food, and tensions between game animals and predators perpetually run high. Forests are peaceful because myriad interconnected actors rely on one another even while they compete.

Mahatma Gandhi said that, "There is no path to peace. Peace is the path." As his words suggest, peace is about making vociferous self-assertions while harboring aspirations. It also comes in the course of expressing concurring and dissenting opinions, and it cannot be obtained by any individual alone. Think of a football match: No matter how much we root for our team, the game will never commence unless we also recognize the opposing side. Peace exists amid the rowdiness of a football stadium.

I believe that peace begins the moment the words "Let's create peace" are uttered. It would be desirable if peace could arrive after a patient, silent wait, but it will not come without action. The possibility of war on the Korean Peninsula was a real concern up until the end of 2017. However, the Korean people wanted peace, and so I sent North Korea a message of peace from Berlin. The North responded positively by participating in the 2018 PyeongChang Winter Olympics, opening the door for multiple inter-Korean and United States-North Korea summits.

Today, the peninsula is witnessing its greatest peacemaking efforts. Even if there are no visible developments, the trend toward peace is flowing vigorously below the surface. Not a single pistol is left in the Joint Security Area, and excavations to find the remains of those who died in the war began after guard posts in the Demilitarized Zone (DMZ) were torn down. So, peace is inching forward.

Nonetheless, more action is needed to achieve peace on the Korean Peninsula. The North Korean nuclear and missile issues have yet to be resolved, and the North is still cautious about engaging fully. North Korea and the US are both demanding that the other take action first. If the North continues to implement denuclearization sincerely, the international community, too, should correspondingly show its efforts. Fortunately, the shared trust between the US and North Korean leaders remains intact, and their commitment to dialogue is unchanged. It is time for actions to be taken in response to actions, and the international community should join forces in this effort.

At the last United Nations General Assembly, I declared three principles for peace on the Korean Peninsula: zero tolerance for war, a mutual security guarantee, and co-prosperity.

Based on these principles, and before the international community,

Through peace, Korea intends to walk the path that ultimately leads to a peace-driven economy."

▼ THE KOREAN DMZ.

I proposed transforming the DMZ across the midriff of the Korean Peninsula into an international peace zone. The DMZ is a colossal green zone that stretches 250 kilometers (155 miles) from east to west and four kilometers from north to south. This tragic space – spawned by 70 years of military confrontation – has, paradoxically, become a pristine ecological treasure trove. It also has become a symbolic space steeped in history, embracing both the yearning for peace and the tragedy of division that is embodied by the Joint Security Area, guard posts, and barbed-wire fences.

I believe that if the international community collectively removes the 380,000 landmines buried in the DMZ, and the UN and other international organizations open offices in the zone, these steps can play the role of a security guarantee on the Korean Peninsula. Transforming the DMZ in this way would institutionally and realistically guarantee North Korea's security and simultaneously bring permanent peace to South Korea. It would serve as an opportunity to help establish a substantive peace regime and achieve denuclearization on the Korean Peninsula while receiving support from the international community.

Korea dreams of becoming a bridging nation. Geopolitically, it is the only country in the world surrounded by four major powers. In the past, the Korean Peninsula was regarded as the periphery of both the continent and the ocean, and sometimes was reduced to an arena in which world powers competed. That was the painful history Korea experienced. But if the Korean Peninsula were to achieve peace, Korea would be in a position to connect the continent and ocean, and lead efforts to establish a peaceful, prosperous order in Northeast Asia. The Korean Peninsula serving as such a bridge would benefit ourselves, Northeast Asia, and the Association of Southeast Asian Nations (ASEAN), as well as the global peace order.

By playing a bridging role, Korea intends to bring about a people-centered community of peace and mutual prosperity. The New Northern Policy is testimony to Korea's continental aspirations. Korea aims to expand the foundation of cooperation to include not only China and Russia but also Central Asia and Europe, and to establish cornerstones for multilateral cooperation and security through the East Asian Railroad Community Initiative. Korea's New Southern Policy, meanwhile, attests to its maritime ambition. This will help elevate Korea's relations with ASEAN and India to the same level as those it has with the major powers surrounding the peninsula, and develop a cooperative partnership of common prosperity with them.

Through peace, Korea intends to walk the path that ultimately leads to a peace-driven economy. Reconnecting severed railroads and roads between North and South is the first step toward becoming a bridging nation that leads peace and prosperity in East Asia. The peace economy will create a virtuous circle where the two Koreas prosper together through economic cooperation with surrounding countries by ushering in an era when division no longer impedes peace and prosperity, which will in turn solidify peace.

Korea has benefited immensely from the international community. It was liberated from colonial rule in the same year that the UN was founded, and later was able to overcome the ravages of war with aid from the UN and the international community. Now, Korea intends to contribute to international peace and prosperity with a sense of responsibility commensurate with its development. The peace economy will expedite humanity's dream of a world in which everyone prospers together.

No matter how desperately peace is desired, Korea cannot afford to race ahead on its own. It has counterparts and must move within the international order. Working-level negotiations and a third summit between North Korea and the US would be the most critical juncture in the entire process of achieving denuclearization and establishing peace on the Korean Peninsula. Support from the international community and concerted actions are needed now more than ever. The wave of peace that began at the PyeongChang Winter Olympics will flow steadfastly into the 2020 Tokyo Summer Olympics and the 2022 Beijing Winter Olympics. In addition, the two Koreas have agreed to cooperate on a joint bid to host the 2032 Summer Olympics. I therefore ask the international community for its support in that regard.

◥ NORTH KOREAN CHEERLEADERS WAVE THE FLAG OF THE UNIFIED KOREAN ICE HOCKEY TEAM.

I am confident that if dialogue and corresponding actions continue, we will need each other more and peace will eventually come. I hope that we can talk more often about peace, advance our respective ideas, and take various actions while moving steadily toward it. It is my hope that the international community will come together and offer unceasing advice until the Korean Peninsula, finally at peace, can shake off the misfortunes spawned by division and conflict, and provide humanity with a new beacon of hope. **18**

Moon Jae-in *is President of the Republic of Korea.*

Toward a New Social Contract

MINOUCHE SHAFIK
*Director of the London
School of Economics*

Every society rests on a web of norms, institutions, policies, laws, and commitments to those in need of support. In traditional societies, such obligations are borne mostly by families and kin groups. In advanced economies, there is a greater burden placed on the state and markets (through health insurance and pensions). Yet even in the latter case, much of the social contract is still upheld by families (through unpaid care work), civil society (voluntary and charitable organizations), and employers, who often must provide health insurance or contributions to unemployment insurance.

THE SOCIAL CONTRACT IS NOT SYNONYMOUS WITH THE welfare state. Rather, the welfare state refers to the dimensions of a social contract that are mediated through the political process and subsequent state action, either directly through taxation and public services or indirectly through laws requiring the private sector to provide certain benefits. As such, the welfare state is best understood not as a redistribution mechanism, but as a source of productivity and protection over the course of one's life cycle. As John Hills of the London School of Economics has shown, most people contribute as much to the state as they receive in return.

Nonetheless, much of the anger that has come to define politics in the developed world is rooted in people's sense of having not received what they are owed. Those born into disadvantage feel as though they never had a chance. Those living in rural areas believe that policymakers have overwhelmingly favored cities. Native-born populations fear that immigrants are receiving benefits before they have paid their due. Men sense that their historic privileges are eroding. Older people regard the young as ungrateful for past sacrifices, and the young increasingly resent the elderly for straining social-security programs and leaving a legacy of environmental destruction. All of this distrust and animosity is fodder for populists.

So, too, are the effects of technological change and globalization. As the chart shows, the integration of global supply chains has delivered huge gains to the middle classes in emerging economies and to the top 1% globally; but it has hollowed out the middle and working classes in advanced economies.

The conventional wisdom is that workers in advanced economies have had to sacrifice wages or social protections to compete with emerging-market labor, and that these pressures have intensified as capital has become more mobile. Worse, the social mobility that once made inequality politically tolerable has stalled or declined.

In principle, the provision of adequate insurance against economic displacement should make the pressures from technological change and globalization manageable. But many aspects of today's welfare states are still designed for the old economy, where male breadwinners paid into reliable pensions over the course of a lifetime, while women stayed at home to raise children and care for the young and the old.

For the first time in history, there are now more women in higher education than men around the world. Educated women have fewer children, are more likely to be in paid work, and will increasingly feel tensions between their participation in the labor market and their traditional caring responsibilities. Yet recent research from the International Monetary Fund shows that closing the gender gap has significant benefits for growth. The challenge, then, is to redefine the social contract so that women can make full use of their talents without any loss of social cohesion.

In advanced economies, this tension is at the center of debates about childcare and declining birthrates. Societal aging means that a shrinking working-age population must cover rapidly rising health-care and pension costs. Worse, today's working-age population already has less security than previous generations, owing to the decline of defined-benefit pensions and a lack of access to many employment benefits or training opportunities.

Likewise, climate change represents a breakdown of the intergenerational social contract. In 2019, young people staged massive protests against an economic model that does not take adequate account of the environment. As the evidence of an impending climate disaster mounts, so, too, has support for alternative

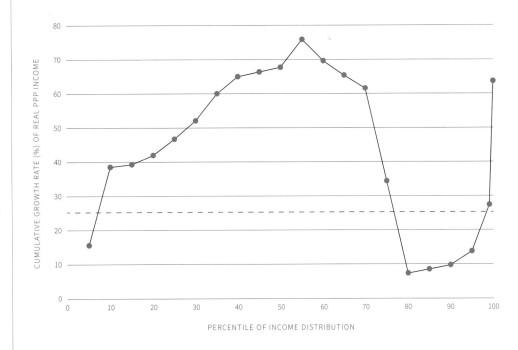

SOURCE: LAKNER, CHRISTOPH; MILANOVIC, BRANKO. "GLOBAL INCOME DISTRIBUTION: FROM THE FALL OF THE BERLIN WALL TO THE GREAT RECESSION." *THE WORLD BANK ECONOMIC REVIEW. VOL. 30:2. PP 203_232. 2016*

economic models that would enable more sustainable development.

Once we have acknowledged these global challenges, we can begin to envision what a new social contract might look like. For example, education will need to occur earlier in life, when the foundation for subsequent learning is established, as well as later, to meet the demand for reskilling. It also will need to focus on tasks that complement what robots can do. Serious investments in reskilling – on the order of 1-2% of GDP, as in Denmark – must be central to any modernized social contract.

A new social contract also may need to provide a minimum income for all, but structured in a way that preserves the incentive to work and retrain. Earned income tax credits, mandatory training and work placements, and employment guarantees should all be considered. And to tap into the world's growing pool of female talent, large investments will be needed to expand childcare and eldercare, provide shared parental leave, and counter the effects of formal and informal biases that place women at a disadvantage. For example, if benefits were made portable and

provided *pro rata*, more workers would be able to rely on part-time work to balance other commitments.

As for sustainability, we need to adopt an entirely different way of thinking about aging and the environment. If a shrinking labor force is going to have any chance of supporting an aging population, the investments needed to boost future productivity must be made now. In the meantime, aging populations may have to commit to working longer – with retirement ages pegged to life expectancy – and demanding less medicalized health care at the end of life. Finally, current and future environmental costs will have to be incorporated into economic decisions. We need massive investments in green technologies to transform cities, transportation, and energy systems. Considered together, such a new social contract has the potential to restore a sense of hope and optimism about the future. **PS**

Minouche Shafik, *a former Deputy Governor of the Bank of England and Deputy Managing Director of the International Monetary Fund, is Director of the London School of Economics.*

Rebuilding the

(De)Reconstruction

THARMAN SHANMUGARATNAM
Senior Minister of Singapore

Political
Center

Although the mass protests in several cities around the world in 2019 erupted spontaneously, they were not bolts from the blue. Trust in either governments or markets to give people a fair chance in life has faded in many countries. Compounding this, a sense of togetherness among people has given way to one of "us versus them."

THESE TENSIONS MANIFEST THEMSELVES differently depending on where one looks. But they reflect underlying realities. Social mobility is stubbornly low in many countries, economic growth has slowed, younger people see fewer prospects of getting good jobs and owning a home, and income and wealth gaps have widened. Globalization and new technologies have contributed to these trends, but they are not at the core of the issue. The few countries that have avoided wage stagnation and the hollowing out of the middle class – Sweden and Singapore, for example – have actually been more exposed to these forces than most. What matters is the policy response, and whether governments, businesses, and unions take responsibility for addressing the difficulties.

The problem is that the loss of trust and solidarity is fragmenting politics and undermining democratic institutions' capacity to muster an effective response. That, in turn, is weakening countries' ability to cooperate to secure global growth, avert crises, and ensure a sustainable world.

The task, then, is to rebuild confidence in the broad center of politics. It requires, most fundamentally, a bolder social ambition. We need more committed and sustained investment in the social foundations of broad-based prosperity if we are to restore optimism in the future. These foundations are in disrepair in much of the advanced world, and woefully inadequate in most developing countries. We must give people a better chance early in life, and second and third chances later, so that no one's path is determined from where they start. And through our politics, and in our schools, neighborhoods and employment, we must develop the sense of affinity among people of different social and ethnic backgrounds that is critical to reducing the appeal of the populist right.

It is much easier to promote relative social mobility when you have absolute mobility, where everyone is progressing. We must ensure this moving escalator continues. When the escalator slows or stops, those in the middle tend to become more anxious not just about those who are moving farther ahead of them, but

◀ FIREFIGHTERS EXTINGUISH A
BARRICADE PLACED BY PROTESTERS
IN DOWNTOWN SANTIAGO.

◢ A HOUSING DEVELOPMENT
IN SINGAPORE.

also about those who might catch up from behind. Reversing the prolonged trend of weak productivity growth and restoring economic dynamism is thus a necessary first step.

But governing from the center must also involve intervening upstream to redress the sources of inequality. We must close the gaps in maternal health and early childhood development, to avoid lifelong disadvantages. We must upskill workers and match them to new tasks while they are on the job, rather than waiting for them to be displaced by new labor-saving technologies. And we must redress the problem of increasingly segregated neighborhoods, which have created growing social distances between people and shaped different aspirations. None of these is easy, but it is far more difficult to tackle the larger problems that form downstream.

These tasks cannot be left to the market, which on its own tends to amplify initial disadvantages and advantages – through assortative mating, better-educated parents investing more time and resources in their kids, hiring practices based on educational or social

pedigree, and the like. It is facile to object to upstream interventions on the grounds that they amount to "social engineering." The state, and all of us collectively, must mitigate the "social engineering" of the market, make opportunities less unequal, and prevent an underclass and other legacies from becoming too entrenched to solve in democratically acceptable ways.

The social contract of the new center must engender both collective solidarity and personal responsibility, transcending the traditional narratives of both the right and the left. The right tends to attribute life's outcomes to whether people take responsibility for themselves. But there has not been any surge in personal irresponsibility that can explain prolonged low productivity and wage growth, the loss of jobs in the middle, or widening regional disparities in so many countries.

Likewise, the left's focus on redistribution as a response to inequality is based on too narrow a view of the state's role and of our collective responsibilities to one another. This view has lost

"But governing from the center must also involve intervening upstream to redress the sources of inequality."

appeal even within the major social democracies. The traditional left would otherwise have performed much better than it did in the aftermath of the 2008 global financial crisis, considering the great difficulties imposed on ordinary working families.

Rather than viewing collective solidarity and personal responsibility as alternatives, we should look for ways in which they reinforce each other. The state and its social partners must broaden opportunities and provide the support that people often need to seize them and earn their own success in education, employment, and contributing to the community themselves. This compact of personal and collective responsibility is what makes strategies for social upliftment succeed. Society never tires of supporting people who are making an effort to help themselves.

When designed well, progressive fiscal systems – taxes and transfers that are fair to the poor and middle class – can support both growth and inclusivity. They are also critical in sustaining support for open, market-based democratic systems. ▶

But the progressivity of the new center must place much greater emphasis on strategies for social mobility, and on helping people, towns, and regions to regenerate themselves when jobs and whole industries are lost. Successful examples of how local networks of public, private, and educational actors have spurred regrowth reflect strategies that seek to empower people, and are fundamentally different from traditional redistributive schemes that "compensate the losers" and which have done little to redress a sense of exclusion.

Part of the solution must also be to refocus attention on public goods. Fiscal policy in many countries has undergone a decades-long drift toward spending on short-term over long-term objectives, and on individuals over the social bases of welfare. To be sure, subsidies for poor and middle-income individuals are essential to ensure fair access to education, health care, and housing, as are policies to top up low wages, such as through negative income taxes. But investments in public goods – efficient public transport, quality public schools, research and development, museums and parks, renewable-energy infrastructure, and the like – are ultimately vital to the quality of life for ordinary citizens, and to restore optimism in the future.

Finally, the new political center must take responsibility for building a more sustainable world, and marshal the energies of the young to help us get there. We cannot keep postponing the large-scale collective action needed to arrest the climate crisis and the already dangerous shifts in the world's ecological balance. To delay any further is to risk crippling consequences for future generations everywhere.

Likewise, we cannot keep pushing the burden of unfunded health-care and pension systems on to the next generation. The new political center must commit to reforms that are socially equitable but sustainable. This requires developing in our democracies the collective capacity to recognize the costs and benefits of our choices. Some societies are developing this capacity, but many have seen an increasing tendency to promise benefits without acknowledging the costs that must be met either today or tomorrow.

Rebuilding confidence in the center will require forging consensus in support of the basic social and political orientations described above. It will take leadership, a strong sense of moral purpose, and agility in today's fragmented political landscapes. But the longer it takes to build this new consensus, the more lasting the damage to both the quality of democracies and to the multilateral order, and the more difficult it will be to restore them. PS

◢ A NEW ELEMENTARY SCHOOL IN FRANCE.

Tharman Shanmugaratnam, *Senior Minister in Singapore's cabinet, is Chair of the Group of Thirty and co-chair of the Advisory Board for the United Nations 2019 Human Development Report.*

Can the World Order Catch Up with the World?

KISHORE MAHBUBANI

*Professor in the Practice of Public Policy
at the National University of Singapore*

The world turned a corner in 2019. The problem is that the world order didn't turn with it. This disconnect could have disastrous consequences. The biggest global change has been the start of the "Asian century." Today, Asia is home to three of the world's top four economic powers (in purchasing power parity terms): China, India, and Japan. The region's combined GDP exceeds that of the United States and of the European Union. ▶

Playing Up

THE US IS NO LONGER EVEN THE MOST GLOBALIZED POWER; THAT title now goes to China. Already a larger trading partner to more countries than the US, China is signing on to more free-trade agreements as well, including potentially the largest in history, the Regional Comprehensive Economic Partnership. The US, by contrast, is abandoning FTAs such as the Trans-Pacific Partnership, which Japanese Prime Minister Shinzo Abe has kept alive without the Americans. The US share of global trade continues to shrink.

The world order has not kept pace with these shifting economic dynamics. On the contrary, the US dollar remains the predominant currency for settling international trade. The US and Europe retain control of the two leading global economic organizations: the International Monetary Fund and the World Bank. And the United Nations Security Council – the only body that can issue binding decisions for the UN's 193 member states – is dominated by just a few, largely declining powers.

In theory, the easiest of these incongruities to address should be the inadequate influence of emerging powers like China in the IMF and the World Bank. After all, the US and Europe have already acknowledged – including in the 2006 and 2007 G20 communiqués – that "the selection of senior management of the IMF and World Bank should be based on merit," ensuring "broad representation of all member countries."

Yet the anachronistic "gentlemen's agreement" that has kept an American at the head of the World Bank and a European leading the IMF has proved stubbornly resilient. In 2007, Dominique Strauss-Kahn became IMF managing director, succeeded by another French citizen, Christine Lagarde, in 2011.

Six years later, Lagarde declared that the IMF could be based in Beijing by 2027, if growth trends continue and are reflected in the Fund's voting structure. After all, she noted, the IMF's bylaws call for the institution's head office to be located in the largest member economy.

"If the Security Council's composition is not updated, the body could lose its credibility and moral authority."

40%

PERCENTAGE OF CROSS-BORDER PAYMENTS SETTLED IN US DOLLARS.

90%

PERCENTAGE OF FOREIGN-EXCHANGE TRADING SETTLED IN US DOLLARS.

Yet, when Lagarde resigned from her post in 2019 to become president of the European Central Bank, it was yet another European who took her place: the Bulgarian economist Kristalina Georgieva. Likewise, the World Bank presidency passed from Robert Zoellick to Jim Yong Kim in 2012, and then to David Malpass in 2019. Future historians will marvel at the imprudence of the old powers' shameless refusal to share control of global institutions.

And yet the US and the EU are not the only ones working to safeguard their clout. In the UN Security Council, the five permanent members (P5) – China, France, Russia, the United Kingdom, and the US – also pay lip service to the need for reform, but consistently obstruct progress. Complicating matters further, additional countries attempting to get a permanent seat on the Council are facing resistance from their neighbors: Pakistan is blocking India's bid; Argentina is blocking Brazil; and Nigeria is blocking South Africa. Given these dynamics, the UN Security Council will be even more difficult to reform than the IMF or World Bank.

But, again, failure could be disastrous. If the Security Council's composition is not updated, the body could lose its credibility and moral authority. If the African Union or India (each with over a billion people) refused to abide by Security Council decisions – essentially the decisions of the P5 – the international community's most important body wouldn't have much recourse.

To avert such an outcome, the Security Council should adopt a 7-7-7 formula. The first seven would be permanent members – Brazil, China, the European Union (represented by France and Germany), India, Nigeria, Russia, and the US – each of which represents a different region. The second seven would be semi-permanent members, a rotating selection of 28 countries, based on population and GNP. The remaining 160 countries would rotate into the remaining seven seats.

The most difficult incongruity to resolve will be that between America's declining leadership and its currency's role as the leading international reserve currency. Today, more than 40% of cross-border payments and 90% of foreign-exchange trading is settled in US dollars. This reflects decades of trust: the US had deep markets, strong institutions – including efficient courts and an independent central bank – and it did not use the dollar as a tool to advance its own interests.

But, since 2017, US President Donald Trump has been aggressively undermining the international community's trust in the dollar. He has pressured the US Federal Reserve to lower interest rates in order to deliver short-term economic growth as he campaigns for re-election. And he has weaponized the dollar, labeling China a "currency manipulator" and instructing the US Treasury to put more countries – including close Asian and European allies – under surveillance.

Trump's behavior has raised the hackles not only of adversaries (Russia leads a new de-dollarization trend), but also of key allies. Jean-Claude Juncker, the former European Commission president, has pledged that the euro would become an "active instrument" of EU sovereignty. It is also telling that France, Germany, and the UK – in collaboration with China and Russia – have created the Instrument in Support of Trade Exchanges (INSTEX) to bypass US sanctions on Iran.

But, in a sense, Trump has done the world a favor by making undeniable what was already obvious. If world leaders do not start addressing the contradictions plaguing the world order soon, the likely result is crisis – and even more dangerous contradictions. ⓟ

Kishore Mahbubani, Professor in the Practice of Public Policy at the National University of Singapore, is the author of Has the West Lost It?

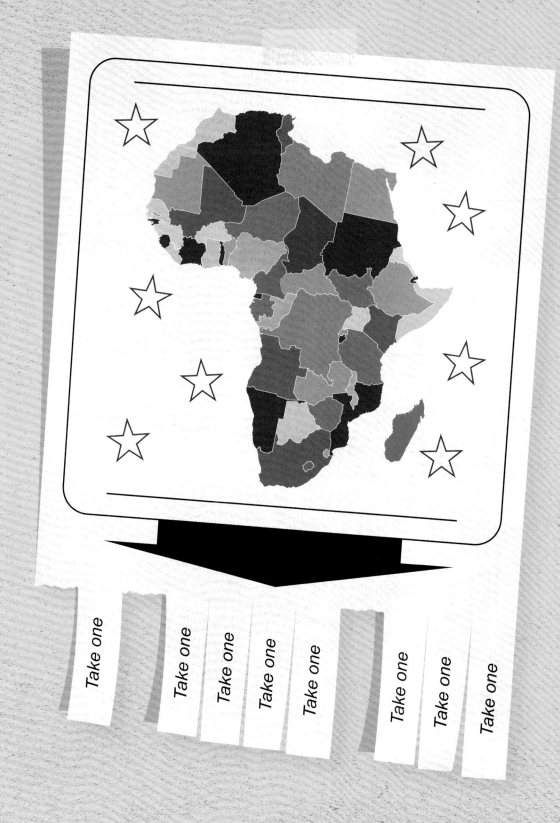

An Agenda for Decent Jobs in Africa

CÉLESTIN MONGA

*Former Chief Economist of
the African Development Bank*

Few people would think that Africa's labor markets are the most dynamic in the world. Yet, according to the International Labour Organization, African countries had some of the lowest unemployment rates in 2018. They include Niger (0.3%), Rwanda (1%), Burundi (1.5%), Madagascar (1.7%), Togo (1.7%), Ethiopia (1.8%), Tanzania (1.9%), Liberia (2%), Benin (2.1%), and Chad (2.2%).

THE REALITY IN THESE COUNTRIES, however, is that almost everyone must work to survive because governments have limited capacity and no fiscal space to support social safety nets. At the same time, African economies also have some of the world's highest *underemployment* rates, owing to erroneous policy choices, low levels of productivity, and insufficient growth, despite the commitment and hard work of an abundant labor force.

Defining unemployment and underemployment, and comparing them across countries, can itself be problematic. According to the ILO, an *unemployed* person is a member of the labor force who was not employed during a specified recent period, and is both available for and seeking work. The *underemployed* comprise the unemployed plus those who are employed part time (less than 30 hours per week) and want to work full time. Yet, although most African economists and statisticians accept the official definitions of these terms, policymakers continue to debate their practical significance.

What is clear, however, is that African *per capita* GDP growth has been insufficient in recent decades – both in absolute terms and compared to other parts of the developing world – and employment has remained overwhelmingly informal.

Africa's rapid population growth poses a further challenge. The United Nations expects the continent's working-age population (those aged 15 to 64) to double to 1.5 billion by 2050, and to reach 2.8 billion in 2100. Providing decent jobs for this massive labor force is perhaps the biggest challenge facing the world – not just Africa. No restrictive immigration policy in Europe or other advanced economies would be able to stop the influx of migrants from a continent burdened by poverty, joblessness, conflict, and the damaging effects of climate change.

The Wrong Approach

Traditionally, developing-country governments have tried to tackle unemployment and underemployment by improving the business environment, typically through reforms aiming to increase labor-market flexibility. This means making it easier for firms to hire and fire workers, scaling back employee benefits, reducing the tax wedge ▶

(the difference between the cost of employing a worker and his or her take-home pay), weakening trade unions, and pursuing active labor-market policies (including employment subsidies and training).

Unfortunately, these conventional measures generally are more appropriate for advanced economies with high levels of full-time employment and relatively expensive labor. In developing economies with far less full-time employment and persistent labor surpluses, these measures rarely produce the hoped-for results. And because traditional policies neglect the most glaring features of low-income countries' labor markets – an acute shortage of good formal sector jobs and widespread informal employment – empirical evidence of their effectiveness is ambiguous at best.

As a recent study from the African Development Bank points out, for too long much of the developing world neglected the key principle of successful job-creation strategies: ensuring that economies develop in a manner consistent with their comparative advantage and are internationally competitive.

Instead of focusing on labor-intensive sectors, African governments often tried to replicate the capital- and technology-intensive industries characteristic of high-income countries. Such a misguided "modernization" drive explains why many African economies remain commodity-dependent and job-scarce six decades after independence.

A Better Way

To circumvent constraints on growth, and boost productivity and job creation, African governments should focus on three policy priorities. First, they need to gear macroeconomic policies toward ensuring external competitiveness – including the adoption of flexible exchange rates to mitigate trade shocks. Economic stability is a precondition for sustained growth and hence the creation of decent jobs, particularly in small developing countries that are most vulnerable to shocks.

Demand-boosting policies play an important role in combating unemployment, especially in economies with good fundamentals. By using fiscal and monetary policies

whenever possible to support economic growth, governments can help to reduce uncertainty – thereby making firms more inclined to invest and hire, even in economies with no lingering excess capacity. Furthermore, macroeconomic policies specifically geared toward job creation make active labor-market programs much more likely to succeed.

Second, therefore, African governments need to consider a range of labor-market initiatives to help create jobs. For example, when fiscal and debt conditions permit, they should accelerate the implementation of carefully designed, labor-intensive public-works programs. Well-targeted public infrastructure projects (whether new investment, repair, or maintenance) provide much-needed incomes, typically to the urban poor, and can help to ease social and political tensions. Moreover, such schemes remove bottlenecks to growth and contribute to increased productivity.

Evidence from Latin American and Caribbean countries suggests that infrastructure investment can have a sizable impact on employment.

Yet, poorly targeted public-works schemes may crowd out some private-sector jobs, so policymakers should set wage levels carefully to ensure that these programs are cost-effective. In addition, governments should refrain from hiring the unemployed directly, but instead contract with private firms or non-profit organizations to provide jobs.

Governments also could consider introducing temporary, transparent, and targeted wage subsidies for industries that are clearly competitive but are facing provisional shocks. Wage subsidies would allow businesses to keep employees on their payroll instead of laying them off, and to hire younger workers and women for a given period while paying part of their salary, enabling them to acquire or develop important skills that eventually could lead to long-term employment.

Because some employers may regard subsidies simply as a temporary means of securing cheap labor, governments must consider the risk of deadweight losses and be prudent in determining the level and duration of support. Furthermore, some regions can be caught in a self-fulfilling

A WOMAN CARRIES STONES AT A GRANITE QUARRY.

◢ THE MONDAY MARKET IN SEMIEN-KEIH-BAHRI, ERITREA.

cycle of dependency in which public-sector jobs become the only source of income, entrepreneurship is discouraged, and the private sector does not develop. That often results in the emergence of powerful political constituencies of public-sector employees and unions that oppose labor-market reforms.

Finally, government-sponsored training programs that help new and unemployed workers to gain or regain skills could boost productivity if they target the neediest segments of society, such as young people, women, and disadvantaged groups. Youth-oriented programs designed in close collaboration with private firms, academic institutions, and nongovernmental organizations can yield good results. To maximize such initiatives' impact, policymakers should tailor them to the needs of potentially competitive industries.

Enclaves of Excellence

African governments' third policy priority should be to establish special economic zones (SEZs) and industrial parks to facilitate the development of sectors with strong competitive potential. Such initiatives help to connect domestic companies to foreign firms and global value chains, and provide platforms for developing capacities and skills. If carefully designed, well-equipped, and managed, SEZs and industrial parks can be enclaves of excellence that attract foreign direct investment, help local small- and medium-size enterprises connect to global value chains, and allow firms to operate efficiently even when the overall business environment is suboptimal.

Of course, African policymakers also must address long-standing problems related to poor investment climates ▶

(De)Reconstruction

91

and weak governance. For example, limited financial resources mean that active labor-market policies in Africa often are either random or politicized, especially with respect to their sectoral and geographic targeting. The presence of vested interests can make it too politically costly to abolish some binding constraints on growth and job creation, such as rigid labor laws. And many African governments currently are unable to afford national public infrastructure programs. Understandably, the reforms needed to remove these obstacles to sustainable economic growth are politically difficult and often take time.

Furthermore, some fear that the so-called Fourth Industrial Revolution will impede the creation of formal-sector jobs in Africa, and thus deprive the continent of its comparative advantage in labor-intensive industries. But such worries are overblown. Robotics and artificial intelligence could help to reorganize workflows in agro-processing, manufacturing, and modern services, thereby creating new labor-intensive activities. Such innovation offers infinite possibilities for Africa.

As US President Franklin D. Roosevelt once said, "The only thing we have to fear is fear itself." By implementing bold policies based on sound ideas, African governments in 2020 can work toward creating enough decent jobs for almost everyone. This would be a major step toward a more prosperous and stable world. PS

Célestin Monga was Chief Economist and Vice President of the Africa Development Bank, 2016–2019.

◀ A TECHNICIAN HOLDS A DRONE USED TO MONITOR A PLOT OF HEAT-TOLERANT HYBRID MAIZE IN ZIMBABWE.

What Next for Emerging Markets?

JIM O'NEILL
Chair of Chatham House

When it comes to the outlook for emerging markets in 2020, the bottom line is maddeningly simple: "It's complicated." There are a number of reasons for this.

FOR STARTERS, WE ARE LIVING IN extraordinary times, owing to the unpredictable personality of the current American president. As the 2020 US presidential election approaches, Donald Trump's behavior is likely to become even more erratic than it already is.

One can only begin to imagine what steps Trump will take to improve his re-election chances. Will he engage in even more saber rattling, threatening, say, additional tariffs against China or military action against Iran? Or will he focus on keeping financial conditions accommodative in order to ward off a slowdown or recession just before the election?

There are no obvious answers to such questions. Indeed, a good friend recently told me that he is closing down his macro hedge fund because the ratio of noise to signal in the Trump era is just too high. Even if one adjusts for the frequency of Trump's outbursts and repeated contradictions, it is impossible to predict where he will land on any given day.

Consider the following story from this summer. During the G7 summit

in Biarritz, France, Trump claimed that he had received calls from China seeking a new round of negotiations to resolve the trade war. But, according to unnamed sources quoted in the US media, this was untrue, and merely an attempt by Trump to prevent stock markets from falling. That tells us a lot about where Trump's ultimate priorities lie. And in the meantime, China and US negotiators have announced a partial trade deal (whether it will last is anyone's guess).

A second complication for the 2020 outlook is monetary policy. What path is the US Federal Reserve likely to take, and what will it mean for the US dollar? These two related issues tend to have a disproportionate influence on developing and emerging markets, particularly those with a lot of dollar-denominated debt.

If the Fed continues easing its monetary policy as expected, and if the dollar stops rising, emerging markets will have less to worry about. But if the Fed is forced suddenly to start tightening – for example, if inflation finally picks up – developing and emerging markets would fare poorly, as would the rest of the global economy, given the cyclical weakness

that has prevailed for most of 2019.

Against this backdrop, one also must consider the underlying structural use of the dollar. Traditionally, the dollar's role in the global economy has been conflated with its price performance against other currencies. But these are now becoming two separate issues, owing to Trump's profligate use of the dollar as a weapon in his various foreign-policy battles. Other countries have taken note of the threat posed by America's "exorbitant privilege," and are now looking for ways to address it.

Russia, for example, has dramatically reduced its US Treasury holdings, and the Europeans have created a payment mechanism for bypassing US sanctions on Iran. Unlike many others, I have long attributed the dollar's dominance to the reluctance of Europe (specifically Germany prior to the introduction of the euro) and China to allow their own currencies to play a bigger role in the global economy. But I would not be surprised if 2019 became the year when these players' attitudes changed.

A third issue, of course, is China, which to my ongoing surprise is still

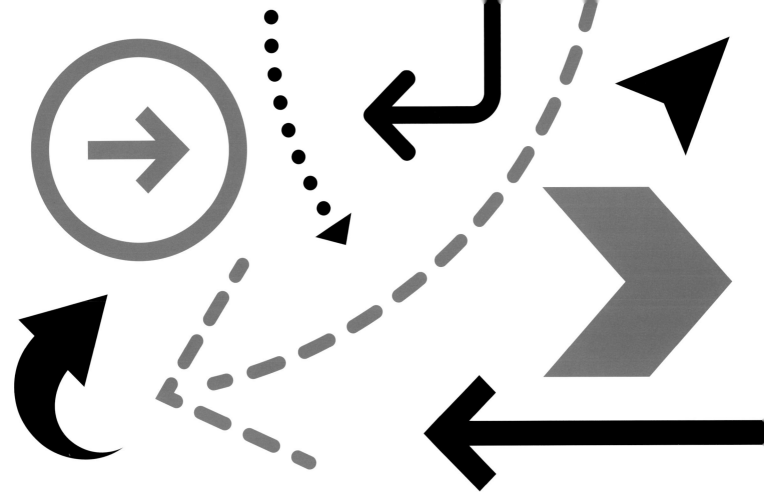

described as an "emerging market." Given China's ever-expanding role in most other countries' economies, it has not fit the traditional definition of an emerging market for quite some time. Still, I suspect that the label will persist as long as China's *per capita* income lags behind that of advanced economies. China already has 4-5 times more people enjoying the same level of wealth as the average British citizen, but it also has almost a billion people who are nowhere close to that standard of living yet.

In any case, the Chinese economy is facing a big complication. In 2020, China's real (inflation-adjusted) GDP growth will likely dip below 6% per year. This will be a major disappointment to all who have grown dependent on a growth rate closer to 7%, and it will be a marginal net drag for many others.

But that is the glass-half-empty view. For those of us who remain focused on China's longer-term growth path, 2020 will likely be the start of a decade during which the country achieves average annual growth of around 5.5%. Indeed, Chinese policymakers cannot expect much more than that, given China's aging labor force.

More to the point, as long as Chinese consumers continue to contribute a growing share of overall GDP, pessimism about China's prospects will be unwarranted. (Needless to say, significantly weaker consumption will be a cause for concern.)

A final issue for so-called emerging markets will be their equity-market valuations. As matters stand, emerging-market equities are generally inexpensive – and, by some measures, quite attractive – relative to equity and bond markets globally. If Trump decides to play nice, the Fed remains a benign influence, and China stabilizes its annual growth rate just below 6%, emerging-market equities could do rather well in 2020.

To be sure, those are major contingencies to consider, and emerging-market countries have plenty of specific challenges of their own. But I would not be too surprised if investors' on-and-off love affair with Sub-Saharan Africa heats up again. Several of those countries are showing signs of positive structural improvement. Investors would do well to keep an eye on them in the coming year. ▮

Jim O'Neill, a former chairman of Goldman Sachs Asset Management and a former UK Treasury Minister, is Chair of Chatham House.

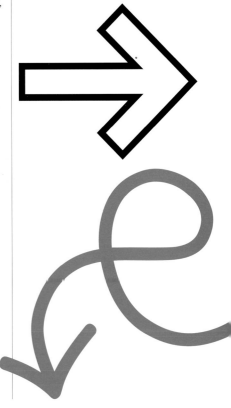

There's More to Life than GDP

MARK CLIFFE
Chief Economist of the ING Group

"Not everything that counts can be counted, and not everything that can be counted counts." This old adage is particularly pertinent as we look ahead to 2020 and beyond. Part of the popular backlash against political and business elites may simply be that people feel the elites are not really focused on what matters to them. But while the single-minded obsession with maximizing market output and profits is being challenged, a more meaningful replacement is not yet in clear view.

GROSS DOMESTIC PRODUCT HAS LONG been the preeminent metric for measuring the size and success of national economies. It is the key target of economic policy, closely watched by politicians, economists, businesses, and investors. But GDP is also deeply – and increasingly – flawed.

Widely regarded as a reliable and objective benchmark, GDP is actually a complex statistic shaped by a history strewn with errors, unresolved controversies, and changing methods and definitions. The core problem is that GDP is not a measure of economic welfare, but rather of output. Its architect in the 1930s, the economist Simon Kuznets, would have preferred to place greater emphasis on welfare. But the US government had tasked him with devising a metric that could guide fiscal policy and shape taxation and spending decisions, so that is what he did.

The result was a statistic focused solely on market-based activities, based on final goods and services to avoid the double-counting of intermediate inputs like raw materials. Yet non-market activities, such as home care and housework, contribute to welfare. Likewise, some market activities harm welfare: think of negative side effects of production such as pollution. Moreover, normative judgments have driven multiple changes in the definition of GDP over the years. Notably, government services, and later financial services, were eventually deemed productive and valuable, and so were added to the definition of GDP. Remarkably, none of this has stopped GDP being widely used as a measure of welfare.

But the problems don't stop there. Another issue is how to account for inflation, given that rising prices can boost nominal GDP even when the volume of output hasn't increased. Measuring output has become increasingly tricky as the mix and features of products and services evolves ever more rapidly.

Consider the complications posed by digitalization, embodied in smartphones, which have little in common with the mobile phones of just a dozen years ago. Statisticians have been trying to account for the advent of smartphones ▶

That's your bloody GDP. Not ours."

(and the relative demise of cameras, calculators, portable music players, and other devices) by adjusting prices to reflect quality changes, but, in the process, they are making a distinction between market prices and value, that is, their contribution to wellbeing.

A related problem is that more money does not always make people happier. In part this is because people are concerned about their status and may be content with less money so long as they have more than others. As such, the distribution of GDP, not just its total, also matters for national welfare. Or as one woman put it in response to an economist's warnings about how Brexit might reduce the UK's output: "That's your bloody GDP. Not ours."

Yet another problem is that GDP does not take account of future prosperity. If current output comes at the expense of future output, future welfare may be jeopardized. True, statisticians do calculate Net Domestic Product by accounting for depreciation (wear and tear) of physical assets. But NDP still tells only part of the story. To get a fuller picture of the sustainability of economic activity, one would also need to account for investments in human capital and the adverse effects of resource depletion.

If it is true that "you manage what you measure," these problems with GDP are particularly troubling, because they are liable to distort government policy and economic decisions. Moreover, if we accept that GDP is not a measure of welfare, we have to ask whose interest it is really serving.

To be sure, GDP at least has an established infrastructure of statistical collection, and its market focus is useful for fiscal decision-making. Moreover, while GDP can be distorted in various ways, there are economists who doubt that such distortions are growing over time. In their view, GDP may be flawed, but it is still the best indicator of national prosperity that we have.

After all, GDP has maintained its dominant position largely because there are no ready-made alternatives without shortcomings of their own – many involving conceptual questions, such as what an aggregate measure is actually for. Is it to measure household welfare? To capture changes in sustainable national wealth? Other issues are more practical:

◤ HOUSING ESTATE IN ROCHDALE, UK.

◣ NOBEL LAUREATE ECONOMIST SIMON KUZNETS.

Do we have the right data? Are we missing forms of capital, such as intangibles and natural endowments?

But whatever the drawbacks, GDP's obvious flaws – and the public backlash against GDP-obsessed elites – suggest that a suite of alternatives is needed. Ironically, while digitalization has made GDP all the more difficult to measure, it could also facilitate the creation of alternatives. The explosion of data collection – some of it real-time and geolocated – that we are now witnessing could open up many new measurement possibilities.

There is a parallel here to the growing range of indicators for corporate performance. Quarterly and annual profit figures once came in a plain vanilla, standardized form. Now, they come in a wide variety of flavors, and are supplemented by a range of additional indicators of balance-sheet health. Moreover, the Business Roundtable, an organization of American CEOs, announced a seminal shift in August by committing to delivering value not just to shareholders, but also to customers, employees, suppliers, and communities.

This is not the first time that the corporate sector has pledged to look beyond short-term profitability. But as we enter 2020 – amid a climate that is deteriorating both literally and figuratively – businesses and politicians alike will be under intense pressure to improve societal welfare. To succeed, they must first figure out how to count what counts. ⓟⓢ

Mark Cliffe is Chief Economist of the ING Group.

The Need for a Global Trade Makeover

DANI RODRIK

Professor of International Political Economy at Harvard University

US President Donald Trump's on-and-off trade war against China added ominous clouds of uncertainty to the world economy in 2019, raising the prospect of a significant global economic downturn. His erratic and bombastic style made a bad situation worse, but the US-China trade war is a symptom of a problem that runs much deeper than Trump's atavistic trade policies.

Fortunately, Democratic candidates in the US presidential race have begun to produce good ideas on which a new trade edifice can be built."

TODAY'S IMPASSE BETWEEN THESE TWO ECONOMIC giants is rooted in the faulty paradigm that I call "hyper-globalism," under which the priorities of the global economy receive precedence over the priorities of the home economy. According to this model for the international system, countries must maximally open their economies to foreign trade and investment, regardless of the consequences for their growth strategies or social models.

This requires that national economic models – the domestic rules governing markets – converge considerably. Without such convergence, national regulations and standards will appear to impede market access. They are treated as "non-tariff trade barriers" in the language of trade economists and lawyers. China's admission to the World Trade Organization was predicated on the assumption that China would become a market economy similar to Western models.

This has clearly not happened. Meanwhile, in the United States and many other advanced economies, hyper-globalism has left behind communities devastated by offshoring and imports – creating fertile ground for nativist political demagogues to thrive. US trade policy has long been shaped by corporate and financial interests, enriching those groups while contributing to the erosion of middle-class earnings. It is now clear that we need a new narrative on trade, one that recognizes globalization is a means to national prosperity, not an end in itself.

Fortunately, Democratic candidates in the US presidential race have begun to produce good ideas on which a new trade edifice can be built. In particular, Senator Elizabeth Warren's trade plan solidifies her credentials as the Democratic candidate with the best policy ideas. Her plan represents a radical reimagining of trade policy in the interests of society at large.

We live in a world where import tariffs are, for the most part, already quite low. Trade negotiators spend most of their time arguing not about import tariffs and other barriers at the border, but about behind-the-border regulations such as intellectual property rules, health regulations, industrial policies, and the like. Trade agreements that target these areas can foster higher levels of international trade and investment, but they also ▶

◥ CHINA JOINS THE WORLD TRADE ORGANIZATION ON NOVEMBER 11, 2001.

encroach more on domestic social bargains. They constrain countries' tax and regulatory policies and their ability to uphold their own social and labor standards. Unsurprisingly, major multinational enterprises such as pharmaceutical companies and financial firms seek access to foreign markets at the expense of the needs of labor or the middle classes.

A key plank of Warren's plan is to establish prerequisites before the US signs deep-integration agreements. Any country with which the US negotiates a trade agreement must recognize and enforce internationally recognized labor standards and human rights. It must be a signatory to the Paris climate agreement and international conventions against corruption and tax evasion. Of course, on labor and the environment, the US itself falls short of meeting some of these preconditions, and

Warren has committed to fixing these "shameful" shortcomings.

This approach is vastly superior to the current practice of assuming trade partners will raise their standards once a trade agreement is signed. In reality, side agreements in labor and environment have proved quite ineffective. The only way to ensure that such issues are treated on par with questions of market access is to restrict trade agreements to countries that are already committed to high standards.

Moreover, some of the most harmful elements in trade agreements should be removed or weakened. Warren rightly proposes eliminating investor-state dispute statement (ISDS) – the controversial practice of allowing foreign corporations to sue governments. She also seeks to limit the scope of monopoly

Nothing in the historical record suggests that poor countries require very low or zero barriers in advanced economies in order to benefit greatly from globalization."

rights in intellectual property, pledging never to push another country to extend exclusivity periods for prescription drugs.

The transparency of trade negotiations needs to be dramatically increased as well. Currently, draft agreements are kept secret until presented for a vote by Congress. Under Warren's proposal, drafts would be open to public scrutiny and comment. Secrecy, combined with the requirement of an up-or-down legislative vote, may have facilitated trade liberalization – on the shallow integration model – in the past. But since the 1990s, they have served to empower corporate lobbies and produced unbalanced deals.

Warren is also ready to impose a "border carbon adjustment," to ensure domestic companies that pay the full social cost of carbon are not disadvantaged by foreign companies that do not. Furthermore, trade agreements would be evaluated not only by their national effects, but also by their regional consequences. Warren would seek congressional approval only after regional, labor, consumer, and rural advisory committees all give their assent.

Focusing on the US, Warren has little to say about the multilateral trade regime and how to reform it. Another Democratic presidential candidate, Beto O'Rourke, has taken this task head-on. He proposes updating WTO agreements to tackle new issues such as currency manipulation, to adopt enforceable labor standards, to revise dispute settlement procedures, and to make "sustainable development" an explicit goal of the multilateral trade regime.

One criticism of Democrats' tougher line on trade is that it will have adverse effects on poorer countries' growth prospects. But there is no inherent conflict between trade rules that are more sensitive to developed countries' social, environmental, and equity concerns and economic growth in developing countries. Nothing in the historical record suggests that poor countries require very low or zero barriers in advanced economies in order to benefit greatly from globalization. In fact, the most impressive export-oriented economic take-offs to date – Japan, South Korea, Taiwan, and even China – all occurred when import tariffs in the US and Europe were at moderate levels, and higher than they are today.

But it is not just the US and other advanced economies that need more policy space. China and other countries should not be encumbered by global trade rules in deploying their own growth-promoting structural diversification policies. Ultimately, a healthy and sustainable world trade regime would be one of "peaceful economic coexistence," in which different economic systems prosper side by side rather than being pressured to conform to a single mold favored by international corporations. ⅌

Dani Rodrik, Professor of International Political Economy at Harvard University's John F. Kennedy School of Government, is the author of Straight Talk on Trade: Ideas for a Sane World Economy.

A Better World Starts at Home

KLAUS SCHWAB
*Founder and Executive Chairman
of the World Economic Forum*

In 2020, the world will mark the 75th anniversary of the liberal international order. Most agree that this framework – comprising the United Nations, the International Monetary Fund, the World Bank, and other multilateral institutions – needs to be updated to address the challenges of climate change, widening inequality, and slowing economic growth. But global-level reform will not be possible without first building more cohesive and sustainable societies. And one way to do that is through "citizens' assemblies" of the kind pioneered by Ireland and other countries.

IN 2019, SEVERAL CRUCIAL international institutions once again proved ill-equipped for today's challenges. The European Union remains paralyzed amid the United Kingdom's torturous Brexit process. The Trump administration has sidelined the World Trade Organization by blocking appointees to the WTO's dispute-settlement body. And the UN suffered a major setback when Chile pulled out of hosting the COP25 climate conference.

These examples suggest that our ability to marshal collective responses to major challenges is under threat. But reforming any one multilateral institution will not fix the problem if its member states – and the communities they represent – remain divided along political, social, and economic lines. After all, the Brexit crisis is not about EU decision-making in Brussels; it is about polarization in the UK. The WTO's crisis stems from gridlock in Washington, DC, and disagreement among member states over how to update the rules of trade. And the last-minute cancelation of COP25 was a consequence of social unrest in Chile, not a lack of enthusiasm among international leaders.

Rather than focusing on the pinnacle of the global-governance pyramid, we should be tending to the fractures in its base. And yet, in many countries around the world, divisions among voters have made it increasingly difficult for political leaders to implement reforms. Voters are increasingly polarized, and politicians who try to find common ground are often punished at the ballot box.

Ireland offers a promising model for escaping this catch-22. For decades, abortion was political kryptonite for Irish policymakers. But then Ireland tried a sociopolitical experiment that is fit for our age of division: it convened a citizen's assembly to devise abortion legislation that a broad base of voters could support.

The Irish assembly selected 99 citizens (and one chairperson) at random to convene a body that was "broadly representative of society as reflected in the Census, including age, gender, social class, regional spread, etc." As such, it achieved a much wider diversity of views than one finds in the established political system. But the assembly also followed rules ▶

that were designed to foster unity. As in many parliaments, members had an equal opportunity to speak, and all deliberations were public. But from the start, members also pledged to respect each other's viewpoints, and to sit at the same table as those with whom they disagreed.

The public closely followed the assembly's proceedings, creating a unique sense of broad-based political participation. People cared deeply about the topic being discussed, but they also learned to appreciate the views held by those on the other side of the table or TV. Ultimately, the assembly issued recommendations, including legalizing abortion, which were then put to the public in the form of a referendum. Many of its proposals are now law.

If we want to overcome political divisions elsewhere in the world,

> [Citizens' assemblies] cannot replace democratically elected legislatures, but they should supplement them when needed."

we should champion this citizen-assembly model. By design, deliberative gatherings of ordinary citizens – whose primary task is to reach agreement, rather than get re-elected – can bypass political antagonism and move toward pragmatic solutions to specific issues. They cannot replace democratically elected legislatures, but they should supplement them when needed.

Similar "stakeholder" approaches have helped elected leaders confront major challenges in other cases. In France, the "yellow vest" protesters (gilets jaunes) softened their tone once President Emmanuel Macron organized a "Grand Debate" for citizens to engage directly in town hall-style meetings across the country. In Belgium, a recent gathering of stakeholders in Antwerp produced a resolution to settle disagreements

▶ FRENCH PRESIDENT EMMANUEL MACRON DURING 2019'S "GRAND DEBATE."

A PRO-CHOICE
MURAL IN DUBLIN.

We must move
quickly if we
are to solve the
major challenges
of our time."

over a major infrastructure project
after decades of inaction. And in
Gdansk, Poland, a citizen assembly
achieved what Tin Gazivoda of the
Open Society Initiative for Europe
describes as "binding changes in
city policy on flood mitigation, air
pollution, civic engagement, and
the treatment of LGBT people."

Once our societies have become
more united around at least some
common ground, it will be easier to
create momentum toward solving
international problems. When people
are satisfied and optimistic about
the direction of their life at home,
they are more willing to take on the
larger challenges that they share
with people elsewhere in the world.
Here, too, we should apply some of
the same principles: international
governance should reflect the
diversity of international society,
not just elites or other select groups.

This, then, is my wish for 2020:
That we mend national- and local-
level divisions through citizens'
assemblies, and that we bring the
same stakeholder approach to our
international institutions. We must
move quickly if we are to solve
the major challenges of our time,
from climate change and rising
inequality to slowing growth and
new concentrations of power – all
of which threaten the wellbeing
of citizens everywhere. ▮

*Klaus Schwab is Founder and
Executive Chairman of the
World Economic Forum.*

The World's Opinion Page

Project Syndicate was established in the early 1990s as an initiative to assist newly independent media in post-communist Central and Eastern Europe. Expansion to Western Europe, Africa, Asia, and the Americas quickly followed, as publishers worldwide sought access to the views of leading thinkers and policymakers on the day's most important global issues.

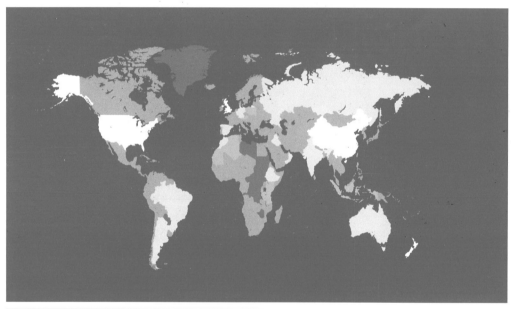

1   PROJECT SYNDICATE'S NETWORK OF MEMBER PUBLICATIONS   13

1,178
WE DISTRIBUTED 1,178 COLUMNS IN 2018.

157
IN 157 COUNTRIES.

534
BY 534 CONTRIBUTORS.

23,575
IN 2018, PS COMMENTARIES WERE PUBLISHED 23,575 TIMES IN OUR MEMBER PUBLICATIONS.

OUR RAPID GROWTH HAS BEEN GUIDED BY RIGOROUS editorial independence and a simple credo: all people – wherever they live, whatever their income, and whatever language they use – deserve equal access to the highest-quality analysis, from a broad range of perspectives, of the events, trends, and forces shaping their lives.

Project Syndicate thus provides an invaluable global public good: ensuring that news media in all countries, regardless of their financial and journalistic resources – and often in challenging political environments – can offer readers original, engaging, and thought-provoking commentary by the world's leading innovators in economics, politics, health, technology, and culture.

Without *Project Syndicate,* most of the publications we serve would be unable to secure comparable content. *Project Syndicate's* unparalleled range and caliber of opinion, our ability to provide analysis of breaking news, and our commitment to focusing minds on complex topics driving the news – development, Asia, Africa, and sustainability, among many others – now benefits some 300 million readers of more than 500 media outlets in 157 countries. PS